STONEWALL KITCHEN

GRILLING

STONEWALL KITCHEN

GRILLING

Fired-Up Recipes for Cooking Outdoors All Year Long

BY JONATHAN KING, JIM STOTT & KATHY GUNST

Photographs by Jim Stott

CHRONICLE BOOKS

SAN FRANCISCO

Library of Congress Cataloging-in-Publication Data available.

ISBN 978-0-8118-6870-9

Manufactured in China.

Design by Katie Heit
Prop styling by Andrea Kuhn
Food styling by Catrine Kelty

10 9 8 7 6 5 4 3 2

Chronicle Books LLC
680 Second Street
San Francisco, California 94107
www.chroniclebooks.com

DEDICATION

To our family, friends, employees, and our dedicated customers
—J.K. and J.S.

To John, Maya, and Emma
—K.G.

ACKNOWLEDGMENTS

We were lucky to have an amazing team working on this book. The photography shoot
was two weeks of cooking over two grills (one charcoal and one gas), shooting hundreds
of pictures, and styling all that grilled food into these gorgeous shots. It all turned out
to be so much fun, we almost forgot it was work. Many thanks to Catrine Kelty, our food
stylist, who made all the grilled foods look so gorgeous; Andrea Kuhn, prop stylist, for her
impeccable taste; Tom Sherman, grill master, who came in from Chicago and got his fill of
Maine lobster; John McNeil, assistant photographer, for his great eye; and Kim Gallagher,
assistant food stylist, for all her help.

We are grateful to Amy Treadwell, our editor and visionary, and to Peter Perez for his
marketing genius. Thanks to our agent, Doe Coover, for schlepping up to Maine over and
over again and helping us make the books we always wanted to make.

TABLE OF CONTENTS

CHAPTER 3
Desserts

INTRODUCTION

Grilling looks like a no-brainer. You light a fire, get it good and hot, and throw some food on the grill. What's the big deal, right? There *is* much simplicity in grilling, but the difference between perfectly grilled food and food that is just thrown on a fire is significant. *Stonewall Kitchen Grilling* aims to set the record straight: Good grilling is fun, simple, and delicious, but—like many things in life—requires patience.

We've been grilling for years. We've always been pretty good at it. But after months and months of cooking, testing, reading, and research, we were amazed to learn how many different types of food can be grilled successfully— from traditional steaks, chicken, ribs, and fish to unexpected ingredients like whole turkeys, pork roasts, bread, lobsters, and even olives and cheese. We grilled every sort of vegetable we could get our hands on. We even experimented with fruit like peaches, figs, pineapples, bananas, and mangoes and were thrilled with the results. In fact, we found that everything tasted delicious when cooked on a grill.

Patience is required when you grill—from the very first step. Whether you're working with charcoal, gas, or wood, you need to start your fire ahead of time and let the grill get hot. A hot grill is the answer to good grilling. But many foods—delicate seafood, ripe tomatoes, peaches, squash, and even chicken—cook too quickly for flavors to really peak when they're cooked over very high heat. That's when you want to use something called *indirect grilling*, where you make a hot fire on each end of the grill. The middle section—where there is no direct fire or heat—is where you cook more delicate foods. (See "Don't Be So Direct: A Simple Guide to Indirect Grilling" on page 37.) Long, slow-grilled foods like brisket, big cuts of beef and pork, whole chickens and turkeys, and even lobsters are also best cooked using indirect heat.

DON'T TRY TO RUSH THE PROCESS. ENJOY BEING OUTDOORS. ENJOY THE PRIMAL SCENT OF WOOD OR CHARCOAL MINGLED WITH THE FRESH FLAVORS OF YOUR DINNER BEING RELEASED INTO THE AIR.

No matter what you're cooking, working with a clean grill is essential. You'll need to clean your grill each time you use it so that last week's steak doesn't flavor tonight's grilled swordfish (see page 42 for more on clean grills). And then you want to make sure you have all the necessary ingredients (equipment, marinades, herbs, salt, pepper, oils, etc.) outside, near the grill, and ready to go. Make sure you have a good working timer so that you can keep track of the cooking times and not have to run back into the house or keep checking your watch. (See "Tools of the Trade" on page 26 for more on getting organized.)

Then it's time to cook. Most grilled foods are traditionally seared—which simply means that the food is cooked entirely over hot heat to seal in the flavors and juices. But then we learned through much trial and error that grilled foods taste really delicious when they are cooked a bit more slowly and carefully. We still sear them over high heat first, but then finish cooking over lower, less intense heat. Again, *patience*. Don't try to rush the process. Enjoy being outdoors. Enjoy the primal scent of wood or charcoal mingled with the fresh flavors of your dinner being released into the air.

Grilled food takes on distinct flavor from the cooking process. We try to provide minimal interference. What this means is that you have to force yourself to stop poking and prodding your grilled foods. Every time you poke and prod something on the grill, you lose precious juices. Let your food grill undisturbed, gently flip it, and let it cook some more. Follow the recipes and the times given. We worked hard to get it right. If you're really unsure about whether a piece of food is properly cooked or not, you can follow our guide (see "Is it Done?" on page 102).

:::::

Americans like to think we invented grilling, but the truth is that cooking food over an open fire is as old as mankind. As you stand outside, inhaling those primitive odors, think back to the first man or woman who thought to make a fire and cook over it. Grilling is a huge part of the world's cuisines—from Latin America, the Caribbean, Southeast Asia, and Australia to the Mediterranean, South America, and the American South. We've tried to incorporate some of the world's best flavors in these grilling recipes, borrowing from cuisines around the globe. When you try our Tuscan-Style Chicken Under a Brick (page 91), Grilled Japanese-Style Eggplant (page 125), Vietnamese Beef Sandwiches with Daikon-Carrot Slaw (page 81), Marinated Skirt Steak with Chimichurri Sauce (page 74), or Italian-style Grilled Swordfish with Olive-Scallion Salad (page 116), you'll quickly see how easy it is to incorporate the best herbs, spices, and flavorings from around the world into grilled foods at home.

:::::

"IT'S TOO OFTEN THAT WOMEN ARE THE COOKS IN THE FAMILY. BUT WHEN IT COMES TO BARBECUE IN AMERICA, IT'S A MAN'S REALM. I'M NOT SURE IF THAT'S A GOOD THING," JIM NOTES, "BUT IT DOES GET ANOTHER PART OF THE FAMILY INVOLVED WITH COOKING, AND I GUESS THAT'S A POSITIVE DEVELOPMENT."

Zen-like" approach to cooking. "I love how patient you have to be," he explains. "There's nothing better than real slow-smoked meats that take all day to cook."

All three of us grew up grilling. Jonathan has vivid childhood memories of his mother taking him and his five siblings to summer at a campground in Cape Neddick, Maine. "Almost every single dinner was cooked on the grill the old-fashioned way over charcoal briquettes. Mom and Dad grilled everything from fresh-caught bluefish and local clams to thick, juicy steaks. Vegetables were tucked into aluminum-foil pouches and placed on the outer edges of the grill.

"Cooking on the grill," he recalls, "was more necessity than a treat. I guess my parents had no idea how fashionable they were when they grilled a whole chicken! Today, I still grill a majority of my meals, many just like when I was a kid."

Jim talks with passion about grilling and barbecuing foods as "an almost

Jim's favorite meal, however, is a plain-old grilled hamburger. "When I was growing up, my mom would use cheaper cuts of meat on the grill and they always tasted great. Hamburgers were flame broiled, literally. I remember neighbors calling up, worried that our house was on fire.

"It's too often that women are the cooks in the family. But when it comes to barbecue in America, it's a man's realm. I'm not sure if that's a good thing," Jim notes, "but it does get another part of the family involved with cooking, and I guess that's a positive development."

There's no better segue to Kathy's story than the issue of sexism and the grill. "When I was growing up, my dad was always in charge of the barbecue," she recalls. "He doused the briquettes with that awful, toxic lighter fluid, flames rushing into the sky, while we kids would scream with delight. He would grill burgers, hot dogs, and thick juicy steaks nearly every weekend from April through November. It was ritualistic; it was a primal activity. Other than grilling, though, my dad didn't get involved much in the preparation of food."

It's not a huge surprise that Kathy's husband, John, has been "in charge" of the grill at her house. "I like to think of our family as being very equal. I do some traditional 'male' jobs and John does many things that could be considered 'female' chores. So it came as a shock to me to realize that we had this real sexist divide when it came to grilling. As soon as we started work on this grilling book, everything changed. I found that grilling could be hugely creative and relaxing. It gets you outside, working with live fire. Not to mention all those fabulous smoky scents!"

We hope *Stonewall Kitchen Grilling* opens up your grilling experience. Try something new and different on your grill tonight. And then try something else. Before you know it you'll be cooking all your meals outdoors—year-round and loving it.

—Jonathan King, Jim Stott, and Kathy Gunst

CHAPTER

SALADS, SIDE DISHES

&

SAUCES

THREE-ONION SALAD WITH CRUMBLED GOAT CHEESE AND BALSAMIC VINAIGRETTE

SERVES 4 TO 6

The colors and textures of these three types of onions—red and yellow onions and leeks—make a gorgeous salad. When onions are grilled, their pungent flavors mellow and they become sweet and slightly smoky. Here, they are grilled until almost soft and slightly charred and then served with crumbled creamy goat cheese, fresh basil, and a light balsamic vinaigrette. We like to use a coarse sea salt in the vinaigrette for flavor and texture.

INGREDIENTS

1 medium-large red onion (about 8 ounces)

1 medium-large yellow onion (about 8 ounces)

5 tablespoons olive oil

2 large leeks, root and tough green ends trimmed, cut in half lengthwise

Sea salt

Freshly ground black pepper

2 ounces chilled goat cheese

2 tablespoons chopped fresh basil or opal basil

2 tablespoons balsamic vinegar

1. Preheat the grill for high direct heat, 400 to 450 degrees F. Place a clean grill rack on the grill and let it get hot for about 3 minutes.

2. Peel the onions, being careful to keep the root ends attached, and cut them into 4 wedges. Drizzle 2 tablespoons of the oil over the onions and leeks and season well with salt and pepper.

3. Cover and grill the onions and leeks for 5 to 8 minutes, or until almost soft and lightly charred. The leeks will probably be done first, at about 5 minutes. Larger (and less fresh) onions can take up to 8 minutes to soften.

4. Arrange the leeks in the center of a large bowl or serving plate. Alternate the yellow and red onion wedges around them. (The salad can be made several hours ahead of time up to this point. Cover and refrigerate until ready to serve.)

5. Crumble the cheese on top of the vegetables and sprinkle with the basil. Drizzle the remaining 3 tablespoons of oil and the vinegar on top of the salad and season lightly with salt and pepper before serving.

GRILLED CAESAR SALAD WITH PARMESAN CHEESE TOASTS

SERVES 2 TO 4

Slightly smoky, with a refreshing crunch, this salad is a fascinating balance of textures. Crisp romaine leaves are very lightly grilled and served with thin shavings of Parmesan cheese and thin toasts coated in anchovy oil and cheese. The vinaigrette, made with anchovies and lemon juice, adds a light, tart, salty balance.

INGREDIENTS

THE VINAIGRETTE

3 anchovy fillets

Sea salt

¼ cup olive oil

3 tablespoons freshly squeezed lemon juice

Freshly ground black pepper

: : : : :

1 large head romaine

2 tablespoons anchovy oil (see Notes)

1 tablespoon olive oil

8 slices baguette or crusty bread, cut about 1 inch thick

3 ounces Parmesan cheese, very thinly shaved (see Notes)

1. *Make the vinaigrette:* In a small bowl, mash the anchovies with just a tiny pinch of salt. Add the oil, lemon juice, and pepper to taste and whisk until smooth. The vinaigrette can be made several hours ahead of time.

2. Preheat the grill for medium-high direct heat, 325 to 375 degrees F. Place a clean grill rack on the grill and let it get hot for about 3 minutes.

3. Rinse the lettuce thoroughly, being careful not to separate the leaves or uncore the lettuce head.

Dry thoroughly. Drizzle 1 tablespoon of the anchovy oil and the olive oil over the lettuce to evenly coat.

4. Brush the bread slices on both sides with the remaining 1 tablespoon anchovy oil.

5. Put the lettuce on the grill rack and cook for about 1 minute on each side, or until the outside leaves are just charred and beginning to wilt, but the inside leaves are still crisp. You can peek by using tongs to reveal the inner leaves. Remove from the heat.

6. Place the bread slices on the grill grate for 30 seconds. Flip the toasts over and scatter half the cheese on top of the toasts, cover the grill, and grill for 1 minute more, or until the cheese is just melted. Remove from the grill.

7. Trim the root end of the lettuce and leave the head whole or cut it in half lengthwise. Place the lettuce in the center of a large plate or small platter.

Arrange the cheese toasts around the lettuce. Scatter the remaining cheese on top of and around the lettuce and spoon a tablespoon or two of the vinaigrette on top; serve the remaining vinaigrette on the side.

NOTES

Anchovy oil is the oil that the anchovies are packed in inside tins and jars.

To shave the cheese, use a wide vegetable peeler and shave off thin slices.

VARIATIONS

Cut 1 or 2 fennel bulbs into quarters, brush with 1 tablespoon olive oil, and grill for about 3 minutes on each side over a hot grill, or until almost tender. The fennel should still have a slight crunch. Serve the grilled fennel surrounding the grilled lettuce.

ASIAN-STYLE CUCUMBER SALAD

SERVES 4 TO 6

This salad is all about light, refreshing flavors that provide a great balance to grilled foods. Best of all, the whole thing takes about ten minutes to put together. It's great with the Beef Satay (page 85), but it goes equally well with the Grilled Beef Tenderloin (page 78), Boneless Pork Roast with Chili-Fennel-Rosemary Rub (page 65), Jamaican Jerk Chicken (page 99), grilled seafood, and more. The salad only needs to sit for about ten minutes, so it can be put together just before serving.

INGREDIENTS

1 large or 2 medium cucumbers (about 10 ounces), peeled and thinly sliced (see Note)

1 large or 2 small shallots, very thinly sliced

2 scallions, very thinly sliced (white and green parts)

¼ cup rice wine vinegar or cider vinegar

1½ tablespoons sugar

Sea salt

Freshly ground black pepper

Red chile flakes

Put the cucumbers in a bowl and toss with the shallots and scallions. Add the vinegar, sugar, and salt, pepper, and chile flakes to taste. Let sit for 10 minutes and up to 1 hour or so. Serve cold or at room temperature.

NOTE
If the cucumber is very large, cut it in half lengthwise and then into thin slices.

GRILLED SUMMER SQUASH SALAD WITH TOMATOES AND LEMON-MINT VINAIGRETTE

SERVES 4 TO 6

We love using a variety of summer squash—zucchini, yellow, and pattypan—for this salad because it adds great color and texture to the final dish. The squash is cut into long, thin slices (lengthwise), lightly brushed with olive oil and thyme, and grilled until tender. The juicy, raw, chopped tomato plays off the grilled squash flavors, and the topping is a refreshing, light vinaigrette full of fresh mint and lemon.

This salad is excellent served with the Grilled Butterflied Lamb (page 69), Tuscan-Style Chicken Under a Brick (page 91), or burgers, or can be served for a light lunch with crusty bread and several good, ripe cheeses.

INGREDIENTS

THE SALAD

2 pounds summer squash (zucchini, yellow, and/or pattypan), cut lengthwise into ½-inch-thick slices

2 tablespoons olive oil

2 tablespoons finely chopped fresh thyme or lemon thyme

Sea salt

Freshly ground black pepper

2 medium-large tomatoes (red, yellow, green, or a combination) or 2 cups cherry tomatoes, coarsely chopped

THE VINAIGRETTE

¼ cup olive oil

1 large lemon, juiced (about 3 tablespoons)

1½ tablespoons chopped fresh mint

Sea salt

Freshly ground black pepper

Fresh mint sprigs, for garnish (optional)

1. *Make the salad:* Preheat the grill for high direct heat, 400 to 450 degrees F. Place a clean grill rack on the grill and let it get hot for about 3 minutes.

2. Place the squash slices on a large plate or broiler pan and drizzle both sides with the oil, thyme, and salt and pepper to taste.

3. Place the squash on the grill rack or directly on

Continued...

…continued

the grill perpendicular to the grate so the pieces don't fall through. Cover and grill the squash for 4 to 5 minutes on each side, or until just tender and with golden brown grill marks. Remove the squash to a plate.

4. Arrange the squash slices and chopped tomatoes alongside each other on a medium salad or serving plate.

5. *Make the vinaigrette:* In a small bowl, whisk together the oil, lemon juice, mint, and salt and pepper to taste until well combined. Spoon the vinaigrette over the squash and tomatoes just before serving, and garnish with the mint sprigs, if desired.

VARIATIONS

Crumble feta cheese or cotija cheese on top of the salad.

Sprinkle the salad with edible flowers like nasturtium or calendula petals.

Grill small onions, shallots, or leeks, peeled and cut in half, until tender, about 8 minutes. Thinly slice and place over the squash.

ALL-AMERICAN POTATO SALAD

SERVES 6 TO 8

This is the classic side dish for barbecue, ideal to serve with virtually any grilled meat, poultry, fish, or vegetable dish. We like Yukon gold potatoes because they are so creamy and hold their shape well, but use whatever waxy potato is local. Make the potato salad at least an hour before serving to give it time to chill.

INGREDIENTS

3 pounds Yukon gold or other waxy potatoes, peeled and cut into 1-inch cubes

½ cup mayonnaise

⅓ cup white wine vinegar or white balsamic vinegar

¼ cup olive oil

½ cup finely chopped fresh parsley

1½ tablespoons finely chopped fresh tarragon or thyme

Sea salt

Freshly ground black pepper

6 large or 7 medium stalks celery, chopped

1. Bring a large pot of lightly salted water to a boil over high heat. Add the potatoes and cook for 10 to 15 minutes, or until just tender when tested with a small sharp knife. It's important that the potatoes not be overcooked or they will become mushy; they will continue to cook a bit once they are drained. Drain the potatoes and let cool and firm up for 5 minutes.

2. Meanwhile in a large bowl, mix together the mayonnaise, vinegar, oil, ¼ cup of the parsley, the tarragon, and salt and pepper to taste. When the potatoes have cooled for 5 minutes, gently mix them into the mayonnaise mixture. Let cool thoroughly in the refrigerator before adding the celery and the remaining parsley. Taste for seasoning before serving.

VARIATIONS

You can also use Grilled Rosemary Fingerling Potatoes (page 28) as a base for this potato salad.

Add ¼ cup chopped fresh lovage for an extra celery flavor.

Add a finely chopped hard-boiled egg.

TOOLS OF THE TRADE

The number of gadgets and grill tools on the market can be overwhelming. Do you really need a wok for the grill or four different-sized grill spatulas? We've found that there are really only a few tools we use consistently and much of the grilling paraphernalia is simply marketing. Here are a few of our favorites:

* A long, sturdy **wire brush** for cleaning your grill. There are many styles and varieties of grilling brushes; ideally, you want something with two sides—one that looks like a stiff wire brush and the other that is flat and looks like a big Brillo pad—that will clean your grill before you cook anything. Having a clean grill is crucial to cooking foods that don't burn!

* A **grill rack or tray** is simply a flat tray with some type of perforation that allows air and heat to have contact with your food but protects ingredients from falling through the regular grates on a grill. These racks are inexpensive and terrific for smaller pieces of food—think shrimp, scallops, bell pepper strips, small cuts of chicken, etc. Be sure to heat up the rack while you heat the grill so that when the food is placed on top it is at the proper temperature. You might also consider a **grilling basket** for foods that require higher sides and even more protection from falling into the grill.

* You'll want a pair of **tongs** to use for flipping foods over, moving them from one side of the grill to the other, etc. The worst thing you can do is use a fork (or one of those long barbecue forks) to move food around a grill. Every time you "stab" a piece of food with a fork you lose precious juices. Tongs allow you to move foods without ever losing any juices or flavor.

* **Pizza paddles** (peels) or **wide metal spatulas** are great for moving larger foods from one side of the grill to the other. We use the pizza paddle when grilling pizzas or whole birds like chicken or turkey and find that it makes it easier to control larger foods.

* **Chimney starters** are helpful for getting charcoal fires started quickly and easily. These inexpensive metal cylinders have a wire grate on the bottom and vent holes. They are designed to heat the charcoal in much less time and more efficiently than throwing a handful of charcoal and newspaper into the bottom

of a grill and hoping it will catch. Simply place the charcoal in the tube, stuff a few sheets of newspaper into the bottom grate, light the paper, and in 10 to 15 minutes you'll have hot coals that can be poured out into the grill.

* You'll want to have several **ovenproof mitts** to use for raising and lowering the grill, moving food off the grill quickly, or generally touching anything hot on or near the grill. We like those thin silicone mitts because they can handle very high heat.

* Look for natural-bristle, long-handled **grilling brushes** for mopping marinades and sauces onto foods. You want a long handle so you can brush marinade onto food while it's on the grill without getting too close to the fire and heat. Be sure to clean your brush after each use in warm, soapy water.

* Have a **small timer** that you can keep out by the grill. It's impossible to keep track of cooking times without one. We used to constantly run from the grill into the house to check the clock before we realized how simple it is to have a timer used exclusively for grilling. Be sure to keep the timer covered and out of the weather when you're not using it.

* **Instant-read thermometers** are helpful for taking the internal temperature on roasts, chops, thick seafood steaks, etc. See "Is It Done?" on page 102 for more detail.

* A **plant sprayer** or **water gun** is a great tool to have for putting out flare-ups and small fires that are created when fat or oil drips from the food onto the fire. Look for a small, inexpensive variety.

* **Trays** are great to have on hand so you can have all your ingredients ready to go. Place the foods you want to grill along with any oil, seasonings (salt, pepper, and herbs), marinades, sauces, or toppings in small bowls on your tray so everything is in one place and ready, outside, by your grill.

* Be sure to have **extra matches, charcoal, and a second (full) propane tank** (on hand) so you can grill spontaneously without worrying about running out of charcoal or gas. It's also helpful when grilling at night to have a good **flashlight** to help you see what you're doing!

GRILLED ROSEMARY FINGERLING POTATOES

SERVES 4

Grilling potatoes over an open fire is one of the great treats of summer. Here we lightly flavor the potatoes with good olive oil, fresh rosemary, sea salt, and coarsely ground pepper; wrap them in foil; and throw them on the grill. During the last 5 minutes, we take them out of the foil and place them in a grill basket to give them a gorgeous golden brown skin and fluffy, tender flesh.

You can serve these hot from the grill or at room temperature, or use them as a base for a grilled All-American Potato Salad (page 25). We particularly like serving these with the grilled Pork Loin Stuffed with Prosciutto and Parmesan (page 58).

INGREDIENTS

1 pound small fingerling or new potatoes, or regular large potatoes, cut into small cubes

2 tablespoons finely chopped fresh rosemary

1½ tablespoons olive oil

Sea salt

Coarsely ground black pepper

1. Preheat the grill for high indirect heat, 400 to 450 degrees F.

2. Place the potatoes on a large piece of aluminum foil and add the rosemary, oil, and salt and pepper to taste. Toss well to coat the potatoes. Wrap the foil up and over the potatoes to make a rounded packet.

3. Place the foil packet over the part of the grill with no direct heat and grill for 45 minutes, covered, shaking the foil packet several times during cooking. Open the packet and place the potatoes in a grill basket or on a grill rack over direct heat. Turning the potatoes frequently from side to side, cook for 4 to 5 minutes, or until golden brown on the outside and tender inside.

PROVENÇAL-STYLE GRILLED TOMATOES

SERVES 2 TO 4

Here, we season lush, ripe summer tomatoes with olive oil, chopped fresh basil, rosemary, thyme, and scallions and then grill them until soft and bubbling. We love eating these tomatoes with crusty bread and an assortment of cheeses. They're also excellent served with the Grilled Beef Tenderloin (page 78), or any chicken dish.

INGREDIENTS

3 tablespoons finely chopped mixed fresh basil, rosemary, and thyme

1 scallion, finely chopped

1½ tablespoons olive oil

2 medium or large ripe summer tomatoes, each cut in half horizontally

Sea salt

Freshly ground black pepper

1. Preheat the grill for high indirect heat, 400 to 450 degrees F. Place a clean grill rack on the unheated part of the grill and let it get hot for about 3 minutes.

2. Divide the herbs, scallions, and oil between the tomatoes and lightly pack onto the tops. Sprinkle with salt and pepper. Place the tomatoes on the hot grill rack; cook, covered, for 7 minutes for large tomatoes and closer to 5 or 6 for medium tomatoes. The tomatoes are ready when they have softened but not collapsed, and the tops are bubbling with juices. Carefully remove each tomato with a wide spatula (they are fragile) and serve hot or at room temperature.

VARIATIONS

On each tomato half, add:

1 teaspoon of tapenade along with the herbs and oil

2 anchovies, criss-crossed into an "X"

An herb-flavored oil

A light sprinkling of organic lavender

GRILLED MEXICAN-STYLE CORN

SERVES 4

On street corners throughout Mexico, street vendors grill ears of corn until they are tender and charred, and then slather them with a creamy sauce and sprinkle ground chile and cheese on top. The sweet, smoky corn mixed with the creamy cheese and a touch of spice is irresistible. Traditionally a dry crumbly cheese like cotija is used, but you can easily substitute crumbled feta, Parmesan, or a firm ricotta salata.

INGREDIENTS

4 ears fresh corn, shucked

2 tablespoons sour cream

2 tablespoons mayonnaise

Sea salt

Freshly ground black pepper

Pure ground chile, such as cayenne or mild New Mexican

About 1 cup crumbled feta, cotija, Parmesan, or ricotta salata

1. Preheat the grill for high direct heat, 400 to 450 degrees F.

2. Put the corn directly on the grill, cover, and cook for 5 minutes. Gently turn the corn and cook for another 5 minutes, rotating the corn once or twice so it cooks on all sides and becomes tender.

3. Meanwhile, in a small bowl, mix together the sour cream, mayonnaise, and salt and pepper to taste.

4. Remove the corn from the grill and spread each ear with 1 tablespoon of the sour cream mixture. Lightly sprinkle with the chile powder and sprinkle on a heavy tablespoon or so of the cheese. The heat of the corn should just melt the cheese. Serve immediately.

VARIATIONS

Soak a long wooden skewer in cold water for 1 hour. Stick the skewer into one end of the corn cob and grill it as directed. This is a fun way to present, and eat, the grilled corn.

Add finely chopped fresh cilantro on top of the cheese.

Serve with sea salt and lime wedges.

GRILLED PROSCIUTTO-WRAPPED FIGS STUFFED WITH BLUE CHEESE

SERVES 7

This is a simple, fast appetizer to make while the grill is hot and you're getting ready to cook your main course. Prepare the figs several hours ahead of time (cover and refrigerate), place them on the grill for 2 to 3 minutes, and you have a hot, delicious treat.

INGREDIENTS

2 ounces blue cheese, at room temperature

1 tablespoon low-fat milk

Sea salt

Freshly ground black pepper

14 small fresh figs

2 ounces thinly sliced prosciutto, cut into long, thin strips

1. In a small bowl, use the back of a spoon to mash the blue cheese. Add the milk, season with salt and pepper, and combine until smooth.

2. Cut each fig in half lengthwise. Spoon about 1 teaspoon of the blue cheese filling onto one of the fig halves and sandwich it together with the other half. Take a strip of the prosciutto and wrap it around the fig, making sure some of the fig peeks through

the top and the bottom of the meat. The figs can be covered and refrigerated for several hours up to this point.

3. Preheat the grill for high direct heat, 400 to 450 degrees F. Place a clean grill rack or piece of aluminum foil on the grill (be sure to punch a few small holes in the foil) and place the figs on top. Cover and cook for 2 minutes. Gently flip the figs, cover, and cook *Continued...*

...continued

for another minute or two, or until the cheese is melted and oozing and the prosciutto is beginning to crisp up. Serve hot.

VARIATIONS

Simmer 1 cup balsamic vinegar over low heat for 45 to 55 minutes, or until thick enough to coat a spoon. Let cool and drizzle the balsamic glaze over the hot, finished figs.

Use goat cheese or cream cheese instead of blue cheese.

Soak long rosemary sprigs in water for 30 minutes and skewer the wrapped figs onto the rosemary before cooking.

Add ½ cup toasted pine nuts or chopped toasted walnuts or pistachios to the blue cheese mixture.

HELPFUL HINTS

GRILLING TEMPERATURES

You'll notice that many recipes call for foods to be grilled over high direct heat or medium indirect heat. Here is a basic chart that will guide you through a range of acceptable temperatures.

HIGH DIRECT HEAT:
About 400 to 450 degrees F

HIGH INDIRECT HEAT:
400 to 450 degrees F

MEDIUM-HIGH DIRECT HEAT:
325 to 375 degrees F

MEDIUM INDIRECT HEAT:
300 to 325 degrees F

LOW INDIRECT HEAT:
225 to 250 degrees F

DON'T BE SO DIRECT: A SIMPLE GUIDE TO INDIRECT GRILLING

Indirect grilling is a revelation. Here's what it's all about: You light the grill—be it charcoal, wood, or gas—and let it get good and hot. Next comes the "trick." You want to create two heat zones—one very hot and one not so hot. With charcoal (or wood) fires, you want to bank the coals on either side of the grill so that the middle part of the grill has no direct heat beneath it. With a gas grill, simply turn off the middle burner (or one side), keeping the two outside burners (or one side) still burning. By doing this you can move the food around from intense heat to moderate heat so that you can control how fast—or slow—your food cooks.

The real advantage to using indirect heat is that you can sear foods over the high heat area (the zone on your grill that is hottest) and then finish off the cooking process over a slower, less-hot part of the grill. You get the good seared flavor you expect from grilling without overcooking foods or letting them blacken or get burnt. Check the recipes and see which ones work best with indirect grilling. For instance, a thick steak probably doesn't need to be cooked over indirect heat—you want that full heat to flavor and cook the steak quickly and evenly. But a beef brisket or whole chicken or delicate piece of fish wants to be seared and then grilled more slowly and gently. Try it out—you'll notice an immediate difference in the flavor, texture, and quality of all your grilled foods.

INDIAN-SPICED CHICKPEAS

SERVES 4 TO 6

We adore these slightly spicy chickpeas so much that they seem to be replacing potato salad and coleslaw as our favorite side dish to grilled foods. You can make the chickpeas several hours, and up to a day, ahead of time; cover and refrigerate until ready to serve. We particularly like serving this salad with grilled pita bread and the Grilled Butterflied Lamb (page 69) or Boneless Pork Roast with Chili-Fennel-Rosemary Rub (page 65).

INGREDIENTS

2 tablespoons peanut oil

2 tablespoons black or yellow mustard seeds

1/8 teaspoon red chile flakes

1/8 teaspoon ground ginger

Two 15 1/2-ounce cans chickpeas, drained, rinsed under cold water, and drained again

1/2 cup coarsely chopped fresh mint

2 scallions, finely chopped

1/4 cup coarsely chopped fresh cilantro

Sea salt

Freshly ground black pepper

2/3 cup plain yogurt, preferably thick like Greek yogurt

1 teaspoon grated lemon zest

2 tablespoons freshly squeezed lemon juice

1. In a large skillet, heat the oil over low heat. Add the mustard seeds and cook for about 2 minutes, or until they begin to pop. Remove from the heat and add the chile flakes and ginger, stirring well.

2. Put the chickpeas into a large bowl. Pour the hot spiced oil on top and stir well. Add the mint, scallions, cilantro, and salt and pepper to taste; gently stir to incorporate all the ingredients. Add the yogurt, lemon zest, and lemon juice and stir well. Taste for seasoning before serving.

GRILLED CAPONATA

MAKES ABOUT 6 CUPS

We love this classic Italian condiment/salad that combines eggplant, tomatoes, onions, bell peppers, celery, capers, and olives. We thought it would be interesting to grill all the vegetables (except the celery) and see if we could create a smoky, grill-flavored caponata—and it was a huge success! This chunky sauce is great for spooning on grilled slices of French bread (bruschetta) or on top of grilled fish, chicken, pork, or lamb. It's also excellent added to a sharp Cheddar cheese sandwich, in grilled panini, and on top of cottage cheese.

INGREDIENTS

2 medium eggplants (about 1½ pounds), both ends trimmed and each eggplant cut lengthwise into quarters

⅓ cup plus 2 tablespoons olive oil

1 green bell pepper, top cut off, cored, and left whole

1 large red onion, quartered, or 2 small onions, halved

1½ pounds ripe tomatoes, halved

2 stalks celery, chopped

½ cup coarsely chopped pitted green olives

⅓ cup capers, drained

¼ cup white or red wine vinegar

Sea salt

Freshly ground black pepper

1. Preheat the grill for high indirect heat, about 400 to 450 degrees F. Place a clean grill rack on the grill over the direct heat and let it get hot for about 3 minutes. Have three very large pieces of aluminum foil ready.

2. Place the eggplants on the grill rack, flesh-side down, and grill for 3 minutes, covered; gently flip them over and grill for 2 minutes more. Place four pieces of the eggplant on one piece of the foil; drizzle with 1 tablespoon of the oil, and tightly seal. Repeat with the remaining eggplant. Place the eggplant packets over indirect heat and cook for another 8 to 10 minutes, or until the eggplant is very soft. Test with a fork or small, sharp knife; the eggplant should be almost falling apart.

3. Grill the bell pepper and the onion over direct heat for 5 minutes, uncovered, flipping them from side to side so they cook evenly on all sides. Move them to indirect heat and cook for another 5 minutes, until tender. Remove and let them cool.

4. Place the third piece of aluminum foil directly on the grill over direct heat.

Add the tomatoes, cover the grill, and cook for about 8 minutes, or until the tomatoes are softened and the juices are beginning to bubble. Remove from the heat and let cool.

5. When *almost cool,* coarsely chop the eggplants, onion, and bell pepper and put them in a large serving bowl. Coarsely chop the tomatoes in a bowl so you

don't lose any of the juices and then add them to the other vegetables. Gently stir in the remaining ⅓ cup oil, the celery, olives, capers, vinegar, and salt and pepper to taste. Cover the caponata and chill for several hours. The caponata will keep, covered and refrigerated, for several days.

IS IT HOT?

The best way to gauge the heat of your grill is to have a built-in thermometer that gives you the precise temperature. But many grills—particularly older grills—don't come with this feature. There's a very simple trick that will help you gauge if your grill is hot enough. Place your hand a few inches above the grill grate. If it feels like "yikes-my-hand-is-burning-off!" and you can't keep it there for more than a second or two, then the grill is hot and ready to go. If you can keep your hand steady for about 4 seconds before it feels too hot, the grill is at medium hot. And if you can keep your hand over the grill for more than 6 seconds, it's low and not very hot at all.

HELPFUL HINTS

DO I REALLY NEED TO OIL THE GRILL GRATES?

Most grilling books instruct you to oil the grill grates before cooking so that foods won't stick. But we say no—not necessary! Surprised? We were. After months of grilling, we found that if you preheat the grill properly and let it get *really hot*, all you need to do is use a grilling brush to clean off the grill grates thoroughly. And it's much easier to clean and brush your grill when it's really hot, so last week's grilled pork doesn't flavor tonight's grilled seafood. We've never had problems with food sticking when we got the grill hot enough and cleaned it before placing any food on it. Avoid extra oil? Sounds good to us!

PISTACHIO-LIME BUTTER

MAKES ABOUT ½ CUP, OR ENOUGH FOR 1½ TO 2 POUNDS FISH,
MEAT, VEGETABLES, OR POULTRY

Spoon this simple sauce onto grilled fish, chicken, skirt steak, or vegetables during the last few minutes on the grill. We especially love it on top of the Grilled Salmon (page 112).

INGREDIENTS

3 tablespoons unsalted butter

1 teaspoon lime zest

3 tablespoons freshly squeezed lime juice

Sea salt

Freshly ground black pepper

½ cup (2½ ounces) coarsely chopped shelled salted pistachios

In a small saucepan, melt the butter over low heat. Add the lime zest and cook for 1 minute. Add the lime juice, and salt and pepper to taste, and cook for 2 minutes more. Add the pistachios and cook for 2 minutes, until they just begin to smell nutty. Remove from the heat and refrigerate the butter until needed.

GREEN GUACAMOLE

SERVES 4 TO 8

We love the fresh, bright flavor of avocados mashed with scallions, jalapeño, cilantro, lime, and good green olive oil. Guacamole goes well with all sorts of grilled and barbecued foods—from chicken and steak to seafood. It's also a classic accompaniment to chips or raw vegetables.

INGREDIENTS

2 ripe (but not too ripe) avocados

3 tablespoons freshly squeezed lime juice

1 scallion, very finely chopped (white and green parts)

1 tablespoon chopped jalapeño pepper, with or without seeds (depending on how spicy you like it)

3 tablespoons finely chopped fresh cilantro

1 tablespoon good green olive oil

Sea salt

Freshly ground black pepper

Hot pepper sauce (optional)

Cut the avocados in half, remove the pit, and place the flesh in a medum bowl. Using a fork, mash the avocados until almost smooth but still somewhat chunky. Gently fold in the lime juice, scallion, jalapeño, half of the cilantro, and the oil. Season with salt, pepper, and hot pepper sauce (if using). The guacamole can be made about an hour ahead of time; put plastic wrap directly on the surface to prevent browning and refrigerate until ready to serve. Sprinkle with the remaining cilantro just before serving.

VARIATIONS

Add 1 cup chopped raw tomatillos.

Add 1 cup chopped ripe red tomatoes.

Add 1 chopped green bell pepper

Serve with bowls of sour cream and salsa.

GRILLED CORN AND JALAPEÑO SALSA

SERVES 4 TO 6

In August when corn is everywhere, we like to find new, interesting ways to use this favorite summer crop. Here, we grill whole ears of shucked corn and slice the kernels off the cob. We grill a whole jalapeño pepper and toss it and the corn with summer tomatoes, fresh green bell pepper, cilantro, and lime juice. The salsa can have some heat (if you add the seeds from the jalapeño) and is delicious served with the Chile Shrimp with Grilled Mangoes (page 107), Grill-Roasted Whole Chicken (page 96), Grill-Roasted Whole Turkey (page 100), or any meat or fish dish. Of course, it's also excellent with tortilla chips or potato chips.

INGREDIENTS

2 ears fresh corn, shucked

4½ tablespoons olive oil

Sea salt

Freshly ground black pepper

1 jalapeño pepper, left whole

1½ cups chopped fresh tomatoes (about 10 ounces)

1 large green or red bell pepper, seeded and finely chopped

¼ cup finely chopped fresh cilantro

2 tablespoons freshly squeezed lime juice

1. Preheat the grill for high direct heat, 400 to 450 degrees F.

2. Put the corn directly on the grill and brush with 1½ tablespoons of the oil; sprinkle with salt and pepper. Cook, covered, for about 7 minutes, turning the corn from side to side, or until lightly charred. (It will not be fully cooked, though.) Let it cool.

3. Grill the jalapeño for 3 to 4 minutes, or until almost charred on both sides and tender. Let cool.

4. Using a sharp knife, slice the kernels from the cobs into a large bowl. Cut the jalapeño down the center and remove the seeds or keep some or all of them, depending on how spicy you want the salsa. Finely chop the jalapeño and add it to the bowl with the corn. Gently toss the corn kernels and jalapeño with the tomatoes, bell pepper, cilantro, lime juice, and the remaining 3 tablespoons oil. Taste for seasoning before serving.

GRILLED PEACH AND PEPPER SALSA

MAKES ABOUT 2 CUPS

Fresh summer peaches—lightly grilled until the juices just begin to caramelize—are mixed with grilled jalapeño peppers, crunchy yellow (or red) bell peppers, scallions, and parsley. The grilled flavor is subtle, but the grilling helps the sugars caramelize and the salsa is sweet and deliciously spicy.

This salsa, a riot of summer colors, textures, and flavors, is delicious served with chips, as a topping for bruschetta, or as a condiment with grilled meat or fish. We also love serving the salsa with sharp cheeses and crusty bread or spooning it onto a cheese quesadilla. The salsa will keep, covered and refrigerated, for a day.

INGREDIENTS

2 large ripe (but not overly ripe) peaches, cut in half and pitted

1 jalapeño pepper, left whole

1 large yellow, red, or green bell pepper

2 scallions, finely chopped

¼ cup finely chopped fresh parsley

2 tablespoons olive oil

1½ tablespoons freshly squeezed lemon juice

Sea salt

Freshly ground black pepper

1. Preheat the grill for high direct heat, 400 to 450 degrees F. Place a clean grill rack on the grill and let it get hot for about 3 minutes.

2. Place the peaches, skin-side down, on the hot grill rack and cook, covered, for 3 minutes. Place the jalapeño on the grill and cook for 2 minutes. Flip the jalapeño over and cook for another 2 minutes, or until the skin is just charred on all sides. Remove and let it cool for a few minutes. Flip the peaches over, flesh-side down, and cook for another 3 minutes, or until they have nice grill marks and are just softening. Remove the peaches from the grill and let them cool for a few minutes.

3. Peel off the skin from the jalapeño. Cut the jalapeño in half and remove the seeds or keep some or all of the seeds, depending on how spicy you like your salsa. Finely chop the bell pepper and put it in a medium bowl. Coarsely chop the peaches and add to the bowl. Add the jalapeño, scallions, parsley, oil, lemon juice, and salt and pepper to taste, and gently stir. Taste for seasoning. Serve cold or at room temperature.

VARIATIONS

Substitute fresh cilantro for the parsley.

Substitute lime juice or red wine vinegar for the lemon juice.

MANGO SALSA

This is a refreshing salsa, full of gorgeous colors, textures, and flavors. Serve with the Pork Loin Stuffed with Prosciutto and Parmesan (page 58), Jamaican Jerk Chicken (page 99), or Grilled Swordfish with Olive-Scallion Salad (page 116). It's particularly good with the Chile Shrimp with Grilled Mangoes (page 107).

INGREDIENTS

2 ripe mangoes, cut into ½-inch cubes

1 small sweet red or yellow bell pepper, seeded and finely diced

1 ripe red or yellow tomato, finely diced

3 tablespoons freshly squeezed lime juice

2 tablespoons chopped scallions (white and green parts)

2 tablespoons finely chopped fresh cilantro

2 tablespoons olive oil

1 tablespoon grated or minced peeled fresh ginger

Pinch of sea salt

Dash of hot pepper sauce

In a medium bowl, gently mix all the ingredients together. Taste for seasoning and add more salt or hot pepper sauce as needed. The salsa can be made several hours ahead of time; cover and refrigerate until needed.

CHIMICHURRI SAUCE

MAKES ABOUT 1 CUP

A mixture of parsley, mint, capers, scallions, lemon juice, and olive oil, this is a cross between a tart salsa verde and a classic Argentinean chimichurri sauce. Serve with the Grilled Vegetable Platter (page 123) or any of the grilled chicken, pork, fish, or beef recipes. This sauce can also be used as a marinade for meat or fish.

INGREDIENTS

1 cup fresh Italian parsley leaves

½ cup fresh mint leaves

2 scallions, chopped (white and green parts)

¾ cup olive oil

¼ cup capers, drained

1 tablespoon freshly squeezed lemon juice

Sea salt

Freshly ground black pepper

About ¼ teaspoon red chile flakes

Put the parsley and mint in the container of a food processor and pulse once or twice until coarsely chopped. Add the scallions and pulse again. Add the oil, capers, lemon juice, and salt and pepper to taste, and blend until coarsely chopped. Place in a serving bowl and gently mix in the chile flakes to taste. The sauce can be covered and refrigerated for up to a day before serving.

MEDITERRANEAN YOGURT SAUCE

MAKES 2 CUPS

This thick, silky sauce is excellent with the Grilled Vegetable Platter (page 123), Grilled Butterflied Lamb (page 69), and Fish Kebobs (page 109). It will keep, covered in the refrigerator, for at least a day.

INGREDIENTS

2 cups Greek-style yogurt (see Note)

¼ cup capers, drained

3 tablespoons olive oil

2 tablespoons freshly squeezed lemon juice

2 cloves garlic, chopped

1 teaspoon lemon zest

Sea salt

Freshly ground black pepper

Put all the ingredients in the container of a food processor and blend until *almost* smooth. Add salt and pepper to taste. Cover and refrigerate until ready to serve.

NOTE

If you can't find Greek-style yogurt, you can place 2 cups plain whole-milk yogurt in a fine-mesh strainer for 1 to 2 hours or until thickened to the consistency of sour cream or cremé fraîché and use the solids as a substitute.

VARIATIONS

Add 1 cup coarsely chopped toasted walnuts, pistachios, or pine nuts.

Add ¼ cup chopped mint leaves.

Add 1 finely chopped scallion.

Add a pinch of chile flakes.

SPICY PEANUT BUTTER SAUCE

MAKES ABOUT 1 CUP

Thick and creamy, with just a touch of spice, this sauce is excellent served with the Beef Satay (page 85), Tuscan-Style Chicken Under a Brick (page 91), grilled shrimp, or as a dip with chips, raw vegetables, or cooked shrimp.

INGREDIENTS

1 scallion, very finely chopped (white and green parts)

1 tablespoon minced peeled fresh ginger

1 tablespoon minced fresh garlic

2/3 cup smooth or chunky unsalted peanut butter

2 tablespoons soy sauce

2 tablespoons sesame oil

2 teaspoons rice wine or mirin

1/2 to 1 teaspoon Chinese chile paste (see Note, page 54) or hot pepper sauce

Freshly ground black pepper

In a medium bowl, mix together the scallion, ginger, and garlic. Using a soft spatula, mix in the peanut butter. Add 2 tablespoons of water along with the soy sauce, sesame oil, rice wine, 1/2 teaspoon of the chile paste, and pepper to taste. Stir to create a smooth sauce. Taste for seasoning; if you want a spicier sauce, add the additional 1/2 teaspoon chile paste. The sauce can be covered and refrigerated a day before serving.

BEST BARBECUE SAUCE

MAKES ABOUT 3 CUPS

This sauce is silky smooth and is a perfect balance of sweet, sour, salty, and spicy. Spread it on Barbecued Chicken (page 95), Dry-Rubbed Pork Ribs (page 61), Slow-Smoked Texas-Style Brisket (page 76), grilled sausages and steaks, etc.

Make a double batch; it will keep in the refrigerator for at least a week.

INGREDIENTS

2 tablespoons vegetable oil

2 tablespoons minced garlic

2 tablespoons minced peeled fresh ginger

About 1 teaspoon Chinese chile paste (see Note)

About ½ teaspoon Sriracha hot chili sauce or hot pepper sauce (see Note)

½ cup balsamic vinegar

½ cup soy sauce

1 tablespoon Worcestershire sauce

2½ to 3 cups ketchup

¾ cup maple syrup or honey

Sea salt

Freshly ground black pepper

In a medium pot, heat the oil over low heat for 1 minute. Add the garlic and ginger and cook, stirring, for 3 minutes. Add the chile paste and chili sauce and stir; cook for 1 minute. Add the vinegar, soy sauce, and Worcestershire and bring to a gentle simmer; cook for 3 minutes. Add 2½ cups of the ketchup and the maple syrup and let simmer on low for 10 minutes, whisking to create a smooth sauce. Taste for seasoning. If you want a sweeter, more tomato-flavored sauce, add the additional ½ cup ketchup. If you want a spicier sauce, add more chile paste and chili sauce. Season with salt and pepper. Let cool; cover and refrigerate until ready to use.

NOTE
Chinese chile paste and Sriracha hot chili sauce are available at Asian food markets and in the specialty food section of many grocery stores. The chile paste is a thick, bright red mixture of ground chile peppers. Sriracha hot chili sauce is a blend of chiles, sugar, salt, and garlic and comes in a bottle with a rooster on the label.

CHAPTER

MAIN COURSES

PORK LOIN STUFFED WITH PROSCIUTTO AND PARMESAN

SERVES 4 TO 6

This boneless pork loin, stuffed with prosciutto, Parmesan cheese, and freshly chopped rosemary, is coated in olive oil and grilled until juicy and bursting with flavors. Serve it with the Grilled Rosemary Fingerling Potatoes (page 28).

INGREDIENTS

1 boneless loin of pork (rib end, if possible; about 2 pounds)

2 tablespoons finely chopped fresh rosemary, plus 1 long sprig fresh rosemary

Sea salt

Coarsely ground black pepper

1 clove garlic, minced

4 ounces thinly sliced prosciutto (about 6 slices)

1½ ounces Parmesan cheese, cut into thin slices

1 tablespoon olive oil

1. Preheat the grill for high indirect heat, 400 to 450 degrees F.

2. Using a long, sharp knife, cut the pork loin lengthwise almost to the end so it opens up flat like a book, but is not cut into two halves. Season the top and bottom of the pork with the rosemary, salt, and pepper. Sprinkle the bottom half of the pork with the garlic and lay the prosciutto slices on the inside surfaces of the meat and then place the cheese on top of the prosciutto. Close the pork up, pressing both halves together. Place the whole rosemary sprig on top of the roast.

3. Use five 10-inch pieces of butcher string to tie the roast up widthwise at 2-inch intervals. Cut off any excess. (The rosemary sprig should be under the string.) Spread the oil over the top of the pork.

4. Place the pork in the middle of the grill over the area without heat. Cook, covered, for 1½ hours, or until the internal temperature is 155 degrees F. It will continue to rise to

Continued...

…*continued*

160 degrees F once the meat is off the grill. Be sure to insert the thermometer into the thickest part of the pork for an accurate reading.

5. Let the meat sit for 5 minutes before cutting into thin slices to serve.

VARIATIONS

Spread a thin layer (about ½ cup) of fig jam onto the pork before layering with the herbs, prosciutto, and cheese.

Add a layer of basil or sage leaves instead of rosemary.

Spread the bottom of the pork with a thin layer of tapenade or olive puree before layering with the prosciutto, cheese, and herbs.

DRY-RUBBED PORK RIBS WITH BEST BARBECUE SAUCE

SERVES 6

When you take baby back ribs and coat them in a pungent dry rub, cook them over low indirect heat for a few hours, and then place them in a paper bag to settle the juices, what you end up with is nothing short of miraculous. These ribs are so tender they almost fall off the bone, and they burst with flavor. We like to serve them with Grilled Rosemary Fingerling Potatoes (page 28) and the Grilled Vegetable Platter (page 123) or coleslaw.

Although you can make these successfully using a gas grill, we particularly like them cooked over charcoal or a wood fire.

INGREDIENTS

4½ pounds baby back pork ribs

⅓ cup packed light brown sugar

¼ cup chili powder

1 tablespoon ground cumin

2½ teaspoons dried thyme

2 teaspoons dried oregano

1½ teaspoons sweet Hungarian paprika

1 teaspoon ground coriander

½ teaspoon ground allspice

Kosher salt

About 1 cup apple cider or apple juice

2 cups Best Barbecue Sauce (page 54)

1. Pat the ribs dry with paper towels and place them on a large roasting pan or platter. In a small bowl, mix together the sugar, chili powder, cumin, thyme, oregano, paprika, coriander, and allspice until blended. Pat both sides of the ribs with the dry rub, taking care to cover all surfaces with the spice mixture (including the rib ends).

Continued...

…continued

Cover the ribs and refrigerate for 30 minutes to 1 hour.

2. Meanwhile, preheat the grill for medium indirect heat, 300 to 325 degrees F. Bank all the coals on one side of the grill. You can also add mesquite or special fruitwood chips to impart a smoky flavor. If your grill's lid has vents, open the vents over the cool side of the grill to regulate the temperature and keep air coming into the grill; ideally, the inside temperature will hover between 275 and 325 degrees F.

3. Lightly sprinkle the ribs with salt on both sides. Place them, bone-side up and fat-side down, on the side of the grill without the heat. Cook, covered, for 30 minutes. Rotate the ribs, placing the rack nearest to the edge in the middle and vice versa, to avoid burning. Pour about 3 tablespoons of the apple cider into the hollow of each rack of ribs and cook for an additional 15 minutes.

4. After 45 minutes total cooking time, carefully flip the ribs. Drizzle with a little of the cider and cook, basting the ribs with a little more of the cider every 15 minutes or so, for an additional 45 to 75 minutes. When you pierce the middle of the ribs with a small, sharp knife, the meat should feel tender. We find they generally take a total of 2 to 2½ hours cooking time.

5. Transfer the ribs to a large sheet of aluminum foil. Wrap the ribs entirely in foil. Place the package inside a large paper bag and fold the bag a few times to seal it. Allow the ribs to sit (at room temperature) for 30 minutes. Remove the ribs from the bag and the foil and serve with the barbecue sauce at room temperature or warmed up in a saucepan.

6. To reheat, place the ribs (in the foil) on a baking sheet in a preheated 350-degree F-oven for 10 to 15 minutes. You can also reheat them in the foil on a warm grill, but take care not to burn them, as the spices might become bitter.

BONELESS PORK ROAST WITH CHILI-FENNEL-ROSEMARY RUB

SERVES 6

Coat a boneless pork roast with an aromatic spice rub and place it on the grill. It's that simple. Serve with Grilled Mexican-Style Corn (page 32), a big salad, and crusty rolls. If you want a sauce, serve it with the Mediterranean Yogurt Sauce (page 52) or the Chimichurri Sauce (page 50).

INGREDIENTS

One 2½-pound boneless pork roast

Chili-Fennel-Rosemary Rub (page 67)

1. Pat the pork roast dry with paper towels. Spread the rub all over the pork, including the sides; cover and refrigerate for 1 to 8 hours.

2. Preheat the grill for high indirect heat, 400 to 450 degrees F. Place the pork on the hot side of the grill and sear on both sides for about 2 minutes. Transfer the pork to the indirect part of the grill and cook, covered, for about 45 minutes, or until the internal temperature registers 155 degrees F. Remove the pork from the grill and let it sit for 5 minutes before cutting into thin slices to serve.

VARIATION

This is a great dish to make with pork chops as well. Rub four 1-inch pork chops (about 1½ pounds) with the Chili-Fennel-Rosemary Rub or the Rosemary-Coriander-Fennel Rub (page 67) and grill the chops for 5 to 7 minutes per side over high heat. Serve with Mango Salsa (page 49).

SPICE RUBS: THREE MASTER RECIPES

Dry spice rubs are one of the simplest, fastest ways to add flavor to meat and fish before grilling (particularly good when there's no time for wet marinades). Make a double batch and keep the rub sealed in a small glass jar in a cool, dark spot or in the refrigerator or freezer for up to six weeks. Try one of these three master combinations or experiment and create your own version.

Smoked Spanish Paprika–Cumin-Chili Rub

MAKES ABOUT ⅓ CUP

Smoked paprika, called *pimentón picante*, comes from Spain and adds a gorgeous red color and smoky, slightly spicy flavor to foods. Here we mix it with light brown sugar, chili powder, cumin, and sea salt. There's enough rub here for 3 pounds of meat; we particularly like it on steaks (especially skirt, flatiron, or flank steak), ribs, pork (chops or tenderloin), and shrimp. Be sure to coat the meat or fish thoroughly and let the rub set for 20 to 30 minutes before grilling.

¼ cup packed light brown sugar

2 teaspoons Spanish smoked paprika (*pimentón picante*)

2 teaspoons sea salt

1 teaspoon ground cumin

¼ teaspoon chili powder

Combine all the ingredients and seal in a small glass jar.

Rosemary-Coriander-Fennel Rub

MAKES ABOUT ⅓ CUP

This rub is particularly good on pork roasts and chops, chicken, ribs, or salmon. This makes enough for about 2 pounds of meat, poultry, or fish.

2 tablespoons dried rosemary

2 tablespoons coriander seeds

2 tablespoons fennel seeds

⅛ teaspoon sea salt

Generous grinding black pepper

In a mortar and pestle, grind the spices until coarse. Seal in a small glass jar.

Chili-Fennel-Rosemary Rub

MAKES ABOUT ¾ CUP

We love this rub on boneless pork, ribs, lamb, or chicken. The recipe makes enough rub for 3 to 4 pounds of meat.

2 tablespoons fennel seeds

2 tablespoons dried rosemary

½ cup packed light brown sugar

2 teaspoons mild chili powder

1 teaspoon ground ginger

¼ teaspoon sea salt

Coarsely ground black pepper

In a spice grinder or using a mortar and pestle, finely grind the fennel and rosemary. Place in a small bowl and mix with the remaining ingredients. Seal in a small glass jar.

GRILLED BUTTERFLIED LAMB

SERVES 10

There are few grilled foods as deeply satisfying as a grilled butterflied leg of lamb. Ask your butcher to do the butterflying (be sure to keep the bone; you can freeze it and keep it to make a soup or stock this winter); then marinate it for a few hours and throw it on the grill. Serve with warm pita bread, the Indian-Spiced Chickpeas (page 39), Mediterranean Yogurt Sauce (page 52), and a green salad.

INGREDIENTS

One 4½- to 5-pound leg of lamb, butterflied and trimmed of excess fat

1 cup dry red wine

¼ cup soy sauce

¼ cup balsamic vinegar

¼ cup chopped fresh mint, plus sprigs for garnish

2 tablespoons Worcestershire sauce

4 cloves garlic, minced

Sea salt

Freshly ground black pepper

1 to 2 tablespoons unsalted butter

1. Place the lamb in a large, nonreactive bowl or a tightly sealed plastic bag. Pour the wine, soy sauce, vinegar, chopped mint, Worcestershire, garlic, and salt and pepper to taste on top and coat thoroughly. Let the meat marinate in the refrigerator for at least 2 hours and up to 12 hours.

2. Remove the lamb from the marinade and strain into a small saucepan. Preheat the grill for high direct heat, 400 to 450 degrees F.

3. Place the lamb on the grill and cook, covered, for 12 to 15 minutes per side. You can test the meat for doneness by placing an instant-read thermometer into the thickest part of the meat; it should read about 130 degrees F for medium-rare meat. Let the lamb sit off the heat for about 5 minutes, lightly covered in foil, before cutting into slices.

4. While the meat is cooking or resting, simmer the marinade over low heat for 10 minutes. Add 1 tablespoon of the butter off the heat and stir until smooth. For a richer, creamier sauce add another tablespoon butter. Spoon a few tablespoons of the marinade over the meat and serve the rest on the side. Garnish with the fresh mint sprigs.

LAMB-MINT SLIDERS

MAKES 10 SLIDERS

Sliders are all the rage. These mini lamb sliders (mini burgers)—mixed with fresh mint, feta cheese, and chives—are moist and bursting with flavor. To make a mini burger roll, simply use a 2-inch glass or biscuit cutter to cut one out of a regular-sized burger roll. We also like to serve them open faced on half of a mini burger roll. Serve with Mediterranean Yogurt Sauce (page 52) mixed with walnuts and mint and arugula or romaine leaves.

INGREDIENTS

1 pound ground lamb

½ cup crumbled feta cheese

2 tablespoons minced fresh mint

2 tablespoons minced fresh chives

Sea salt

Freshly ground black pepper

10 mini hamburger rolls

1. In a medium bowl, thoroughly combine the lamb, feta, mint, chives, and a generous sprinkling of salt and pepper. Form into 10 small burgers about 2 inches wide and about ¾ inch thick.

2. Preheat the grill for high direct heat, 400 to 450 degrees F. Place a clean grill rack on the grill and let it get hot for about 3 minutes.

3. Grill the sliders for 4 to 5 minutes on each side, covered, without pressing down on them with a spatula. During the last minute, grill the hamburger buns for about 1 minute, or until warm and just beginning to brown. Sandwich the meat with the buns and serve hot.

VARIATIONS

Substitute goat cheese for the feta.

Serve the sliders on pita bread instead of buns. Cut the pita bread as described for the hamburger buns.

Serve the sliders on crunchy croûtes made from any good crusty bread cut into 2-inch rounds and grilled until lightly toasted.

"MEATBALL" SLIDERS

MAKES 12 SLIDERS

The idea here is to take a slider—or mini burger—and give it all the rich flavor and appeal of a meatball, but none of the fuss. We form ground meat, grated Parmesan, fresh sage, egg, and panko breadcrumbs into 2-inch sliders and then grill them over high heat. They are served on crunchy toasted slices of French bread spread with a spicy tomato ketchup, relish, or chutney.

INGREDIENTS

1 pound ground round or sirloin

⅔ cup panko or regular dried breadcrumbs

½ cup grated Parmesan cheese

3 tablespoons minced fresh sage or 1½ tablespoons dried and crumbled

1 large egg

Sea salt

Freshly ground black pepper

12 slices French bread, ¾ inch thick

2 tablespoons olive oil

½ cup spicy ketchup, tomato chutney, or a spicy tomato-vegetable spread like ajvar (see Note)

1. In a large bowl, thoroughly combine the ground meat, panko, Parmesan, sage, egg, and a generous amount of salt and pepper. Work the meat to thoroughly incorporate all the ingredients and form into 12 two-inch sliders.

2. Place the bread slices on a plate and drizzle both sides with the oil.

3. Preheat a grill for high direct heat, 400 to 450 degrees F. Place a clean grill rack on the grill and let it get hot for about 3 minutes.

4. Cook the sliders for about 4 minutes on each side, covered, for medium-rare and up to 6 minutes for well-done. During the last minute, place the oiled bread on the grill for about 30 seconds on each side, or until golden brown and lightly toasted.

5. Place the toast on a large serving plate. Place a burger on the toast and top with 1 teaspoon of the ketchup. Serve hot.

NOTE
You can find spicy ketchup, tomato chutney, and ajvar or lutenica at specialty food shops. You can also simply spike a store-bought ketchup with hot pepper sauce until it is spicy.

MARINATED SKIRT STEAK WITH CHIMICHURRI SAUCE

SERVES 4 TO 6

It wasn't all that long ago when skirt steak was a relatively unknown cut of meat found in French bistros and specialty butchers—but rarely in American grocery stores. Well, times have changed. Skirt steak is the new darling of the meat-eating food world. Skirt is ideal for grilling because it's lined with a thin layer of fat (keeping it moist and very flavorful), and it's not a thick cut, so it cooks up in no time.

This steak is marinated in herbs, garlic, and olive oil, quickly grilled, and served with a pungent chimichurri sauce. Serve with steamed green beans, Grilled Vegetable Platter (page 123), and a salad made with a good variety of garden greens.

INGREDIENTS

2 pounds skirt steak, trimmed of excess fat

¼ cup olive oil

3 tablespoons chopped fresh parsley

2 tablespoons chopped fresh cilantro

1 tablespoon chopped fresh mint

2 cloves garlic, minced

Sea salt

Freshly ground black pepper

Chimichurri Sauce (page 50)

1. Put the steak in a non-reactive bowl and cover on both sides with the oil, parsley, cilantro, mint, garlic, and salt and pepper to taste. Cover and refrigerate for 1 hour and up to 8 hours. Bring the meat to room temperature before grilling.

2. Preheat the grill for high direct heat, 400 to 450 degrees F.

3. Remove the steak from the marinade and pat dry by lightly dabbing the meat with a paper towel. Cover and grill for 3 to 5 minutes per side for medium-rare meat, brushing the marinade onto the meat once or twice while it cooks. Let cool for 1 or 2 minutes before thinly slicing the meat on the diagonal. Serve hot with the Chimichurri Sauce.

SLOW-SMOKED TEXAS-STYLE BRISKET WITH BEST BARBECUE SAUCE

SERVES 6

This is long, slow cooking at its best. We put a dry rub on a beef brisket (look for second-cut brisket, which is a touch fattier and makes a moister, better cut for grilling) and then cook it over an indirect fire set up with small packets of wood chips. The brisket cooks long and slow—2 to 3 hours—and is great piled high on a toasted roll and served with corn on the cob, All-American Potato Salad (page 25), and a good summer salad. Oh, and lots of cold beer and napkins.

INGREDIENTS

1 beef brisket, preferably second cut (about 4 pounds)

1 tablespoon cumin seeds

1 tablespoon sea salt

1 tablespoon peppercorns

2½ tablespoons light brown sugar

1 tablespoon chili powder

About 2 cups Best Barbecue Sauce (page 54)

1. Dry the brisket thoroughly with paper towels.

2. Using a mortar and pestle or a spice grinder, coarsely grind the cumin seeds, salt, and peppercorns. Using a spoon, mix in the sugar and chili powder. Place the brisket on a shallow aluminum tray or a broiler pan and pat half of the spice rub on top. Flip the brisket over and pat the remaining spice rub on the other side. Cover and refrigerate for at least 30 minutes and up to overnight.

3. Preheat the grill for medium indirect heat, about 300 to 325 degrees F. Soak 2 cups of mesquite or other wood chips in a bowl of cold water for 15 minutes. Drain and place inside a double layer of aluminum foil to create two little packets. Using a fork, poke a few holes in the tops of the packets. Place the wood chip packets directly on the coals on either side of the grill or on either side on top of the grate for a gas grill.

4. Place the brisket *in the aluminum tray or broiler pan* in the center of the grill.

Cover and cook the brisket for 2 to 3 hours, or until it has a golden brown color and the meat seems tender when prodded with a small sharp knife. Be sure to baste the brisket with any juices that accumulate in the bottom of the pan. If using charcoal, you may need to add additional coals to each side halfway through cooking to maintain the 325 degree F temperature.

5. Remove the brisket from the heat and let sit for about 15 minutes before carving across the grain. Serve with Best Barbecue Sauce warm or at room temperature.

GRILLED BEEF TENDERLOIN

SERVES 4 TO 6

Beef tenderloin—the king of the beef world—is a long, cylindrical piece of filet mignon before it is cut into individual steaks. The price is scary, but the results are sublime. There are no bones, waste, or fat in this cut. We like to keep it simple to pay homage to the high quality of this meat. We lightly coat the beef in olive oil and then simply pat coarsely cracked pepper, sea salt, and fresh thyme all over the outside of the meat. Then we cook it using the indirect grilling method (see page 37) and let the magic happen! The beef is excellent served with any of the sauces in this book, particularly the Grilled Peach and Pepper Salsa (page 46) and the Chimichurri Sauce (page 50). Serve with a summer tomato salad, asparagus, coleslaw, and the Grilled Rosemary Fingerling Potatoes (page 28).

This recipe calls for a smaller cut, but you can follow this recipe using a larger tenderloin and simply add to the cooking time until you get the internal temperature you desire.

INGREDIENTS

One 2½-pound beef tenderloin, tied

1½ tablespoons olive oil

2 teaspoons coarsely cracked black pepper (see Note)

1½ teaspoons coarse sea salt

2 teaspoons finely chopped fresh thyme or 1 teaspoon dried and crumbled

1. Place the beef on a tray or plate. Rub the oil onto both sides of the beef, coating it all over. Pat half the pepper, salt, and thyme on one side of the beef. Flip the meat over and spread the remaining pepper, salt, and thyme on the other side. Let it sit at room temperature for 15 minutes or in the refrigerator for about 1 hour.

2. Preheat the grill for high indirect heat, 400 to 450 degrees F.

3. Place the meat on the hottest part of the grill and sear on both sides, about 4 minutes per side. Using tongs, move the beef to the side of the grill without direct heat and cook, covered, for *Continued...*

…continued

another 20 to 30 minutes, or until a meat thermometer inserted in the center registers 140 to 150 degrees F for medium-rare. Let the meat sit off the heat for at least 5 minutes before thinly slicing.

NOTE

Use a pepper mill adjusted to a coarse setting to get the pepper coarsely cracked.

Alternately, you can place whole peppercorns in a mortar and pestle or food processor and coarsely crack them.

HOW DO THEY GET THOSE PERFECT GRILLED "X" MARKS?

It's called "crosshatching" and it refers to those perfect little "Xs" you see on restaurant-grilled steaks and chicken. How do they do it? Simple. Place the food—beef, chicken, pork, fish, or even vegetables—on a hot grill. Let it cook for several minutes and then use tongs to rotate the food 90 degrees on the same side and let it cook further. You'll end up with perfect crosshatch marks that will make you feel like a pro.

VIETNAMESE BEEF SANDWICHES WITH DAIKON-CARROT SLAW

SERVES 4

Banh mi may just qualify as the ultimate sandwich. This Vietnamese favorite features skirt steak marinated in a sweet lemongrass-garlic sauce and grilled for just a few minutes on each side. The thinly sliced beef is layered on a crusty baguette spread with a daikon-carrot slaw, slices of jalapeño pepper, fresh cilantro, and mayonnaise.

If you like, you can simply marinate the beef, grill it, then thinly slice it and serve over mixed summer greens tossed with fresh mint leaves and lime wedges, with crusty bread on the side.

INGREDIENTS

THE LEMONGRASS MARINADE

1 large or 2 small stalks fresh lemongrass (see Notes)

5 cloves garlic

2 tablespoons Asian fish sauce (*nuoc mam*)

2 tablespoons sugar

1½ tablespoons soy sauce

1 teaspoon Asian sesame oil

: : : : :

1 pound skirt or flank steak

THE DAIKON-CARROT SLAW

8 ounces daikon, peeled (see Notes)

1 medium carrot, peeled

½ cup rice vinegar or cider vinegar

1 tablespoon sugar

Salt

: : : : :

2 tablespoons vegetable oil

1 tablespoon Asian fish sauce (*nuoc mam*)

1 tablespoon soy sauce

1 crusty baguette, 20 to 24 inches long

2½ tablespoons mayonnaise

½ cup packed fresh cilantro sprigs

Tender lettuce leaves, such as Boston lettuce

Continued...

…*continued*

1. *Make the marinade:*
Remove the outer leaves
from the lemongrass and
discard. Thinly slice the
lower bulb-like half and
save the rest for a soup or
stock. Put the lemongrass
and garlic into the container
of a food processor and
whirl until finely chopped.
Add the fish sauce, sugar,
soy sauce, and sesame oil
and blend.

2. Put the steak in a large
nonreactive bowl and pour
the marinade on, making
sure to coat both sides.
Marinate for at least 1 hour,
and up to overnight.

3. *Make the slaw:* Grate
the daikon and carrot on
the large holes of a cheese
grater and mix in a bowl.
Add the vinegar, sugar, and
a pinch of salt and stir well.
Let sit for about 15 minutes.

4. Preheat the grill for
high direct heat, 400 to
450 degrees F.

5. Grill the beef for 3 minutes per side, covered, or
until still slightly rare.
Remove from the heat
and let cool for 5 minutes.
Cut the beef thinly on the
diagonal.

6. In a small bowl, mix the
vegetable oil, fish sauce, and
soy sauce and set aside.

7. Cut the baguette down
the middle lengthwise and
place it on the hot grill for
about 2 minutes, or until
warm. Place the baguette
halves on a clean work
surface and spoon the fish
sauce mixture on one side
and the mayonnaise on the
other. Sprinkle the cilantro
sprigs on top of the mayonnaise and place the beef

on top of the other side.
Distribute the daikon slaw
on top of the beef, add the
lettuce leaves, and carefully
put the two sides of the
bread together. Cut into four
sandwiches to serve.

VARIATIONS

Substitute peeled jicama
for the daikon.

Serve with hot pepper
sauce.

NOTES

Fresh lemongrass can be
found in the produce aisle
of most supermarkets or
in Asian markets.

Daikon is a large Asian
radish with an exceptionally
sweet, almost juicy flavor.

BEEF SATAY WITH SPICY PEANUT BUTTER SAUCE

SERVES 4 TO 6

Serve these aromatic beef sticks as an appetizer or hors d'oeuvre or as the main course for a light lunch or dinner. The thick, peanut butter–based sauce balances out the beef and creates a wonderful contrast of flavors and colors. Serve with the Asian-Style Cucumber Salad (page 20).

INGREDIENTS

¼ cup soy sauce

¼ cup sesame oil

¼ cup rice wine or mirin

2 scallions, very thinly sliced (white and green parts)

1½ tablespoons honey

1 tablespoon minced garlic

1 tablespoon minced peeled fresh ginger

Sea salt

Freshly ground black pepper

1 pound steak tips, flank steak, or skirt steak, cut on the diagonal ¼ inch thick

Spicy Peanut Butter Sauce (page 53)

1. Soak 6 long (or 8 to 10 small) bamboo skewers in a bowl of cold water for at least 1 hour. This will prevent the skewers from burning on the grill. Drain and let dry.

2. Meanwhile, in a medium bowl, mix together the soy sauce, sesame oil, rice wine, scallions, honey, garlic, ginger, and salt and pepper to taste.

3. Slide several pieces of beef onto each bamboo skewer lengthwise, so very little of the beef hangs over the sides of the skewer (6 to 8 pieces on the large skewers and 3 to 4 pieces on the small skewers) and place in a shallow broiler pan. Pour the marinade on top and let the meat sit for at least 15 minutes and up to several hours. Cover and refrigerate if marinating for more than 15 minutes.

4. Preheat the grill for high direct heat, about 400 to 450 degrees F. Place a clean grill rack on the grill and let it get hot for about 3 minutes.

5. Remove the skewers from the marinade and grill for 3 minutes, covered and

Continued…

...*continued*

undisturbed. Gently flip the skewers over and grill for another 3 minutes, covered. Remove from the grill and serve hot or at room temperature with the peanut sauce.

VARIATIONS

Substitute 1 pound boneless breasts of chicken, cut into thin pieces, and grill for about 4 minutes per side.

Substitute large whole deveined shrimp with the peel on and grill for 3 to 4 minutes per side.

"I'LL TAKE MINE ON A STICK, PLEASE"

Grilling on skewers is a quick, simple way to grill a variety of foods easily. Great examples are Fish Kebobs (page 109), Grilled Greek Salad with Chicken (page 89), and Beef Satay with Spicy Peanut Butter Sauce (page 85). We've found that there are a few simple ways to make grilling with skewers easier:

* Always soak bamboo or wooden skewers in cold water for at least an hour before placing food on the skewers and grilling. If you don't soak them, the skewers tend to burn and can disappear into the fire with your food dangling from a burnt piece of wood.

* Whenever possible, use a separate skewer for each type of food. It's difficult to thread a skewer with five types of food—say a piece of chicken, a tomato, an onion, and peppers—and expect them all to cook evenly. Each ingredient needs to grill for different times and over different levels of heat. We've found that if you place the chicken pieces on one skewer,

the tomatoes on another, and the peppers on yet another, you can control how long each food cooks and end up with everything perfectly grilled. Take a look at our recipe for Grilled Greek Salad with Chicken (page 89) to see how it all works. And it looks beautiful to serve a whole skewer of cherry tomatoes, chicken, or baby onions!

* Think outside the (grill) box—rather than use wooden or metal skewers, think about using all-natural sticks to cook food. If you strip the leaves from thick, woody rosemary stems, they make fabulous skewers (not to mention that they perfume and flavor your food). Imagine marinated lamb pieces grilled on rosemary skewers. Or use slivers of thick lemongrass stems to grill chicken or fish and get a natural lemon flavor inside your food. If you have trouble skewering ingredients on these all-natural skewers, you can use a metal skewer to make a hole in the food and then transfer the food to the rosemary or lemongrass.

* You can also use fresh sugarcane as a skewer. You'll find sugarcane in the specialty food section of gourmet and Asian markets. To cut sugarcane into skewers, you'll need to trim off the ends, peel, and cut into thin strips, about ¼ inch wide and 6 to 8 inches long. Like wooden skewers, be sure to soak herbs, lemongrass, or sugarcane in water for about an hour before skewering the food to avoid burning.

* Use two skewers when cooking shrimp, scallops, fish fillets, or small pieces of meat—to help them stay on the skewer and cook evenly. Simply thread the food between two parallel skewers, making sure the food lies flat between the two.

GRILLED GREEK SALAD WITH CHICKEN

SERVES 4

We love eating cool, refreshing Greek salads all summer long and thought it would be fun to "deconstruct" this classic dish. We marinate chicken breasts in lemon, garlic, olive oil, and oregano (all very Greek flavorings) and skewer them alongside bell peppers, onions, tomatoes, and even olives! Serve the grilled chicken and vegetables on top of either crunchy romaine lettuce or hot couscous with grilled feta cheese "croutons."

INGREDIENTS

1½ pounds boneless, skinless chicken breasts, cut into 2-inch pieces

½ cup olive oil

3 tablespoons freshly squeezed lemon juice

1 teaspoon lemon zest

2 tablespoons chopped fresh oregano or 2 teaspoons dried and crumbled

2 cloves garlic, minced

24 cherry tomatoes

3 large green, red, or yellow bell peppers, or one of each, cut into ½-inch strips

2 medium red or yellow onions, cut into 6 wedges

24 large green pimiento-stuffed olives

Sea salt

Freshly ground black pepper

One 7-ounce block feta cheese, drained and chilled

1 cup panko or regular dried breadcrumbs

4 pita rounds

4 cups chopped crisp romaine lettuce leaves or 2 cups cooked hot couscous

Mediterranean Yogurt Sauce (page 52)

1. Place the chicken in a nonreactive bowl and toss thoroughly with ¼ cup of the oil, the lemon juice, lemon zest, oregano, and garlic. Marinate for at least 1 hour and up to 8 hours, refrigerated.

2. Divide the chicken between two large skewers. Skewer all the tomatoes together, then the bell peppers (skin-side out), onions, and olives. Brush the vegetables with 2 tablespoons of the oil and season with salt and pepper.

Continued...

… *continued*

3. Pat the feta dry with a kitchen or paper towel and cut it into 8 pieces. Place the breadcrumbs in a small bowl. Brush each piece of feta with the remaining oil and coat with the breadcrumbs, pressing down to help them adhere. Refrigerate until ready to grill.

4. Preheat the grill for high direct heat, 400 to 450 degrees F. Place two clean grill racks on the grill and let them get hot for about 3 minutes.

5. Grill the chicken, covered, for about 15 minutes, turning the skewers several times during grilling. The chicken should be cooked through with no sign of pinkness.

6. Grill the bell peppers and onions for a total of about 11 minutes, flipping them halfway through, until soft and charred. Grill the tomatoes for about 7 minutes, flipping them halfway through, until just tender and slightly charred. If the tomatoes start to burst, remove them from the heat. Grill the olives for about 2 minutes on each side or until they start to get grill marks. Place the cheese around the outside of the fire (or on a higher shelf with a gas grill) and cook for about 4 minutes, flipping them once, or until just soft but still intact. Warm the pita breads on the grill for about 3 minutes, or until warm and just beginning to puff up.

7. Place the skewers on a large platter and let everyone help themselves. You can also remove the food from the skewers and serve the hot grilled food on top of a bed of mixed greens or hot couscous. Serve with the warm pita bread and Mediterranean Yogurt Sauce.

TUSCAN-STYLE CHICKEN UNDER A BRICK

SERVES 4 TO 6

The first time you try this classic Italian recipe—a whole chicken is butterflied, marinated, and then grilled with the weight of a very hot foil-covered brick pressing down on the skin—you just might think it's the best chicken you've ever eaten. The skin gets crispy, the meat stays juicy and flavorful, and the overall effect is something like, "Why can't all chicken taste like this?"

Give the chicken a few hours to marinate in the herbs and garlic and oil. The actual grilling time is less than an hour. Serve with an orzo salad; a tomato, mozzarella, and basil salad; and a crusty Italian ciabatta.

INGREDIENTS

1 whole chicken (about 4 pounds), butterflied (see Note)

¼ cup olive oil

2 tablespoons finely chopped fresh thyme

2 tablespoons finely chopped fresh rosemary or oregano

2 cloves garlic, minced

2 teaspoons sea salt

2 teaspoons lemon zest

1 teaspoon coarsely ground black pepper

Sweet Hungarian paprika

1 lemon, cut into wedges

Fresh thyme and rosemary sprigs

1. Place the butterflied chicken in a nonreactive pan or bowl and sprinkle with the oil, thyme, rosemary, garlic, salt, lemon zest, pepper, and a generous sprinkling of paprika. Flip the chicken over and make sure it's coated well with the marinade on both sides. Cover and refrigerate for

Continued...

…*continued*

at least 1 hour and up to 24 hours. Bring the chicken to room temperature before grilling.

2. Preheat the grill for high indirect heat, 400 to 450 degrees F.

3. Cover two clean bricks with aluminum foil and place them over the heat. (If you don't have access to bricks use a heavy, oven-proof skillet.) Let the bricks warm up for about 3 minutes, or until very hot.

4. Remove the chicken from the pan and let the excess oil drip off. You can also blot it dry with a paper towel on both sides. Place the chicken, spread flat and skin-side up, on the hottest part of the grill. Cook for 2 minutes. Using a spatula or tongs, gently flip the chicken over and grill, skin-side down, for 2 minutes. Transfer the chicken, skin-side down, to the part of the grill that has the lower heat, and place the hot bricks on top of the chicken. Cover and cook for 30 to 40 minutes, or until the chicken is tender and the juices run yellow and not pink when tested with a small, sharp knife. Remove from the grill and serve with the lemon wedges and sprigs of thyme and rosemary.

NOTE

Butterflying a chicken is much like butterflying a leg of lamb, where the center bone is removed creating two sides to the meat that open up and resemble a butterfly. In this case you need to ask the butcher to remove the backbone and breast bone (or try it yourself) so the chicken can be spread out flat on the grill, ensuring even cooking.

BARBECUED CHICKEN

SERVES 4

This is the classic, all-American barbecued chicken dish—with improvements. When you slather the grilled chicken with our Best Barbecue Sauce, the raves will roll in. You can also marinate the chicken and grill it without the sauce for a simpler dish.

Serve with All-American Potato Salad (page 25); a chopped tomato, pepper, and cucumber salad; Green Guacamole (page 44) and chips; crusty rolls; and ice-cold beer.

INGREDIENTS

1 whole chicken (about 3 pounds), cut into 8 pieces

2 tablespoons balsamic vinegar

2 tablespoons soy sauce

1 teaspoon minced peeled fresh ginger

1 teaspoon minced garlic

2 cups Best Barbecue Sauce (page 54)

1. Place the chicken in a large nonreactive bowl and cover with the vinegar, soy sauce, ginger, and garlic; toss to coat all the chicken. Cover and refrigerate for 1 hour or overnight. Remove the chicken from the marinade and pat dry. Bring the chicken to room temperature before grilling.

2. Preheat the grill for medium-high direct heat, 325 to 375 degrees F.

3. Grill the chicken pieces for 5 to 10 minutes per side, until the juices run yellow and not pink. The breasts need to cook for about 8 minutes per side; the wings should cook for 6 to 8 minutes per side; and the legs should cook for 8 to 10 minutes per side. During the last 5 minutes of grilling, baste the chicken with 1 cup of the barbecue sauce, spreading it on both sides and letting it cook onto (and glaze) the chicken for 5 minutes. Serve warm or at room temperature with the remaining warm or room-temperature barbecue sauce on the side.

GRILL-ROASTED WHOLE CHICKEN WITH MISO AND GINGER GLAZE

SERVES 4 TO 6

We're not sure why grilled chicken usually refers to chicken cut into pieces and smeared with a thick, sloppy sauce, but here we roast a whole chicken over indirect heat (see page 37), lightly coated in a miso-ginger paste. The whole chicken takes on a gorgeous glaze, and the Asian flavors of soy sauce, sesame oil, and fresh cilantro add a whole new dimension to grilled chicken. Serve with hot rice or a rice salad, Grilled Japanese-Style Eggplant (page 125), and a green salad.

INGREDIENTS

1 whole chicken (3 pounds), trimmed of excess fat

Sea salt

Freshly ground black pepper

Two 1-inch pieces peeled, fresh ginger, plus 3 tablespoons minced peeled fresh ginger

2 tablespoons finely chopped fresh cilantro or thyme

⅓ cup yellow or white miso (see Note)

3 tablespoons soy sauce

1 tablespoon sesame oil

1. Preheat the grill for high indirect heat, 400 to 450 degrees F.

2. Clean the inside and outside of the chicken and dry thoroughly. Season the outside and inside with salt and pepper. Place the 2 ginger pieces and half the cilantro into the cavity of the bird.

3. In a small bowl, mix together the miso, the remaining cilantro, and the minced ginger. Using a pastry brush or your hands, rub the miso mixture onto the skin, spreading it all over the surface of the bird.

4. Place the chicken on the part of the grill without direct heat, cover the grill, and cook for 30 minutes.

5. Mix the soy sauce and sesame oil in a small bowl. Brush the soy and sesame oil mixture onto the bird, coating the entire outside and placing a bit in the cavity as well. Grill for another *Continued…*

...*continued*

30 to 45 minutes, covered, making sure the heat is maintained at around 400 degrees F. The chicken is done when it is a rich brown color on the outside. When you gently jiggle the drumstick, it should feel loose and when you insert a small, sharp knife into the thigh, the juices should run yellow and not pink. Remove from the grill and let sit for about 5 minutes before carving.

NOTE
Miso, fermented soybean paste, is found in Asian markets and in the refrigerated produce aisle of most supermarkets. Many health food stores also sell miso.

TO COVER OR NOT TO COVER?

HELPFUL HINTS

When should you cover the grill and when should you leave it open? Here's one way to think about it: When the grill lid is open, your grill is acting like high heat on a stove top. All the heat is under the food and it is hot and strong and concentrated. You are essentially searing food by cooking it over a direct source of heat. This is ideal with thicker cuts of meat like steak, pork chops, and lamb chops, or thick cuts of seafood. This type of open grilling is ideal when you want to cook food quickly, sear it, and give it a good caramelization on the outside and have a medium-rare center.

When you close the lid of the grill, you are essentially creating conditions that mimic roasting in an oven, a convection oven, or a barbecue pit, where there is heat all around the food and not just under it. Your food will be smoky (when you close the lid, all the smoke swirls around inside the grill rather than outside) and grill-roasted. This method works best when you are using indirect heat (see page 37) and cooking foods that need to cook a bit longer and slower.

JAMAICAN JERK CHICKEN

SERVES 4

Throughout the Caribbean you find the sweet smell of chicken coated in spicy Scotch bonnet peppers grilling over an open fire. Our version of this classic Jamaican dish combines garlic, onions, chile peppers, nutmeg, and allspice ground into a thick paste that coats the chicken for several hours. The chicken is grilled until crisp and juicy, redolent with the flavors of the islands. Serve with a creamy coleslaw and biscuits.

INGREDIENTS

1 small onion, chopped

2 scallions, chopped (white and green parts)

1 large or 2 small cloves garlic

1 Scotch bonnet chile or 2 jalapeño peppers, chopped, with or without seeds (see Note)

1½ teaspoons ground allspice

1½ teaspoons ground nutmeg

1 teaspoon coarsely ground black pepper

1 teaspoon sea salt

¼ cup soy sauce

1½ teaspoons canola oil

1 whole chicken (3 to 4 pounds), quartered

1. Put the onion, scallions, and garlic in the container of a food processor and pulse until coarsely chopped. Add the chile, allspice, nutmeg, pepper, and salt and pulse a few more times to mix well. Add the soy sauce and oil and pulse until well incorporated.

2. Place the chicken in a large nonreactive bowl and pour the marinade on top, making sure to coat the chicken well on both sides. Cover and refrigerate for a minimum of 1 hour and up to overnight.

3. Preheat the grill for medium-high direct heat, 325 to 375 degrees F.

4. Remove the chicken from the marinade, reserving the marinade. Place the chicken on the hot grill and cook, covered, for 15 minutes. Using a barbecue or pastry brush, brush some of the marinade on the chicken. Flip the chicken over and cook, covered, for another 15 minutes. Brush more of the marinade on top and cook for another 10 minutes, flipping and brushing one more time, until the chicken juices run clear. Remove from the heat and serve hot or at room temperature.

NOTE
If you add all the seeds from the chile pepper(s) you will have a *very spicy* marinade.

GRILL-ROASTED WHOLE TURKEY

SERVES 10

This recipe is nothing short of a revelation. Kathy's friend Jane Fletcher brought a grill-roasted turkey to a party and Kathy couldn't believe how juicy, tender, and delicious the meat was. The recipe, it turns out, couldn't be simpler. You put a small (10- to 12-pound) whole turkey over indirect heat with a minimum of seasoning. You walk away. You come back around 2 hours later and there is a picture-perfect glazed turkey with juicy meat and a subtle smokiness. You will not believe how a plain old turkey, simply seasoned with salt and pepper and placed on a hot grill, can have this much flavor with so little fuss!

You can grill the turkey a day ahead of time or make it in the morning and feed a crowd later that day.

Serve with All-American Potato Salad (page 25), Grilled Vegetable Platter (page 123), and the Grilled Summer Squash Salad with Tomatoes and Lemon-Mint Vinaigrette (page 21).

INGREDIENTS

One 10- to 12-pound turkey

Sea salt

Freshly ground black pepper

3 cloves garlic, minced (optional)

3 tablespoons chopped fresh thyme, rosemary, basil, or sage, or a combination (optional)

1. Place a disposable aluminum drip pan directly under the center of the grill to catch all the juices and fat and not create a mess of your grill.

2. Preheat the grill for high indirect heat, 400 to 450 degrees F.

3. Clean the turkey and dry it thoroughly. Season liberally inside and out with salt, pepper, and the garlic and herbs (if using). Place the bird on the part of the grill without direct heat. Cover and cook for about 2 hours, or until the juices in the cavity are yellow, and no longer pink; when you jiggle

the drumstick, it should feel loose. The turkey will cook faster than it will in an oven, so keep an eye on it—particularly during the last 30 minutes of the grilling time. Look for a deep brown crispy skin. You can also test the internal temperature with an instant-read thermometer (see page 102). Remove from the grill and let it sit for 10 minutes before carving.

IS IT DONE?

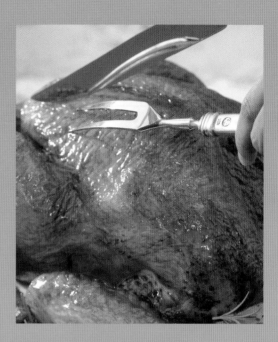

Knowing when grilled foods are perfectly cooked takes some time, experience, and patience. Here are a few tips.

* Many experienced grillers like to simply use their fingers to poke the food to see if it's done. When meat is rare, it will feel soft and yielding. When it's grilled to medium, it will feel slightly resistant. When it's well-done, the food will feel resistant and almost springy. Chicken and turkey can be tested by inserting a small, sharp knife into the thickest part of the meat; the juices should run yellow and clear, and not pink. To test fish, press the thickest section with your finger; the fish should turn opaque and yield and start to flake when done.

* You can also use an instant-read thermometer to test the internal temperature of your food. Keep in mind that temperatures generally continue to rise once food is taken off the grill; remove food when it's 5 degrees below the desired temperature.

* **BEEF AND LAMB:** 140 to 150 degrees F for rare to medium-rare meat and 160 to 165 degrees F for medium to well-done.

* **PORK:** 155 to 160 degrees F for medium-rare to medium and 170 to 185 degrees F for medium to well-done.

* **POULTRY:** Breast meat should be between 160 and 170 degrees F; thigh meat should be 180 degrees F.

GRILLED LOBSTER WITH GARLIC-HERB BUTTER

SERVES 4

Many people are suspicious when we talk about grilling lobsters. Why bother, they ask? They're so good steamed! If you've never grilled lobster outdoors over an open fire, you're in for a treat.

This lobster is cooked over indirect heat (see page 37), allowing the lobster to cook slowly and become moist, slightly smoky, and infused with garlic, herbs, and butter. If you are squeamish about the idea of cutting a live lobster, ask your fish store to do it for you, but be sure to cook the lobsters within an hour or so after they have been cut.

Serve with Grilled Mexican-Style Corn (see page 32) or steamed corn on the cob, All-American Potato Salad (page 25) or Grilled Rosemary Fingerling Potatoes (page 28), a tomato salad, and lots of ice-cold beer or a cold fruity white wine.

INGREDIENTS

6 tablespoons unsalted butter, at room temperature

2 cloves garlic, minced

3 tablespoons chopped fresh chives

2 tablespoons chopped fresh thyme

1½ tablespoons chopped fresh basil or rosemary

Sea salt

Black pepper

Four 1¼- to 1½-pound live lobsters, preferably soft shell (see Note)

1 lemon, cut into wedges

1. Put the butter and garlic in a small saucepan and simmer over low heat for about 4 minutes, or until the butter is bubbling and the garlic has softened. Remove from the heat and add the chives, thyme, basil, a pinch of salt, and a generous grinding of pepper and stir well to mix all the ingredients. The

Continued…

…*continued*

garlic-herb butter can be made several hours ahead of time; cover and refrigerate until ready to cook the lobsters.

2. Preheat the grill for high indirect heat, 400 to 450 degrees F.

3. Meanwhile, place the lobsters on a clean work surface, shell-side down. One at a time, place a tea towel over the lobster's head and plunge a knife into the body, directly below the head, and split the lobster open, cutting it down the middle, *almost* all the way through. The lobster should still be attached and not separated into two halves.

(This technique may seem gruesome, but many experts claim it's more humane than plunging the poor things into a pot of boiling water.) Remove and discard the sac at the top of the head. Alternately, have your fish store cut the lobster for you.

4. Divide the garlic-herb butter between the lobsters. If the butter is still melted, brush it onto the tail and into the body cavity with a barbecue or pastry brush. If the butter is chilled, rub into the body and the tail of the lobsters.

5. Place the lobsters on the side of the grill *without* the direct heat, shell-side down, so that you don't lose any

juices. Cover the grill and cook for about 15 minutes. Remove the cover and cook for another 2 to 6 minutes, depending on the size of your lobsters, until the tail meat feels just firm, and not soft and raw. Remove from the hot grill, place on a platter, and scatter with the lemon wedges to serve.

NOTE
Soft-shell lobster tends to be less expensive than hard shell and is ideal for grilling. Since the shell is softer, it's easier to cut the lobster down the middle. And because the shell is soft, the heat of the grill cooks the lobster more evenly and quickly.

CHILE SHRIMP WITH GRILLED MANGOES

SERVES 4 TO 6

Chinese chile paste, garlic, olive oil, and lemon zest make a fiery marinade for shrimp. The shrimp are then threaded between two skewers so they lie flat and cook evenly, and grilled for a few minutes on each side. Turns out grilled mangoes are absolutely delicious—smoky, juicy, and full of flavor that marries well with the shrimp or any seafood.

Serve with a rice salad, or the Indian Spiced Chickpeas (page 39), a cold noodle salad, couscous, or on top of summer greens. The shrimp are also delicious served with the Grilled Corn and Jalapeño Salsa (page 45).

INGREDIENTS

1¾ pounds shell-on medium shrimp, deveined

3 tablespoons olive oil

3 cloves garlic, minced

1 teaspoon Chinese chile paste with garlic (see Note) or Sriracha hot chili sauce

1 teaspoon Chinese chile paste (see Note), plus ¼ cup for serving

1 teaspoon lemon zest

2 almost-ripe mangoes

2 tablespoons freshly squeezed lemon juice

1 lime, cut into wedges

1. Put the shrimp in a medium nonreactive bowl. Toss with 2 tablespoons of the oil, the garlic, both chile pastes, and the lemon zest and marinate, covered and refrigerated, for at least 1 hour and up to 12 hours.

2. Hold a mango upright on a cutting board and, using a large, sharp knife, cut just over one third of the fruit off the side of the mango. Repeat with the opposite side so you have two large pieces of mango, leaving behind the irregular shaped pit. Use a small sharp knife to score a tic-tac-toe pattern into the fruit, with lines about ½ inch apart. Push the mango skin to make the flesh pop into little squares. (Cut any remaining fruit off the pit and eat!! You only need the two side pieces.) Brush the squares with the remaining 1 tablespoon of oil. Repeat with the second mango.

3. Preheat the grill for high direct heat, 400 to 500 degrees F.

Continued…

…continued

4. Drizzle the lemon juice over the shrimp and toss. There are two ways to skewer the shrimp: Simply skewer them on several long metal or bamboo skewers (see "I'll Take Mine on a Stick, Please," page 86) or place the shrimp between two skewers, threading one end of the shrimp onto each skewer so they are attached. The advantage here is that the shrimp stays flattened and cooks more evenly. Grill the shrimp for 2 to 3 minutes per side, or until golden brown on the outside and cooked through and firm on the inside. To test for doneness, remove a shrimp from the skewer and remove the peel and taste. It should be firm and cooked through.

5. Grill the mangoes, fruit-side down, for 2 to 3 minutes, or until golden brown and just beginning to soften. Serve the shrimp and grilled mangoes with the lime wedges and a small bowl of chile paste on the side for dipping.

NOTE
Chinese chile paste is just ground pure chiles, while the paste with garlic also includes oil and salt. Both are available in Asian markets and in the specialty food or Asian aisle of your supermarket.

FISH KEBOBS

SERVES 6

This is a great party dish because the kebobs can be marinated and put together hours before your guests arrive. We like to use an assortment of fish and vegetables, such as shrimp, scallops, and swordfish, with fresh basil leaves, cherry tomatoes, and bell pepper strips. You can also add onions, thin slices of summer squash, or any other vegetables and herbs you like. The key is to make sure the fish and the vegetables are all cut about the same size so they don't cook at different rates.

Serve the fish kebobs on a bed of couscous, rice, or pasta, or simply serve them alongside a good summer salad. The Grilled Caponata (page 40) is delicious with the kebobs.

INGREDIENTS

12 ounces shell-on medium shrimp, deveined

12 ounces sea scallops

1 pound swordfish, tuna, or any firm-fleshed fish, cut into 1-inch pieces

About 8 ounces cherry tomatoes

1 red, green, or yellow bell pepper, thinly sliced

About 24 whole basil leaves, plus 2 tablespoons chopped fresh basil

6 to 10 thin slices fresh lemon

⅓ cup white wine

2 tablespoons olive oil

Sea salt

Freshly ground black pepper

1. Soak 6 large or 10 small bamboo skewers in cold water for 1 hour before using, to prevent them from burning.

2. Skewer all the seafood and vegetables, alternating them in any order so that each skewer has a good assortment of shrimp,

Continued . . .

…continued

scallops, swordfish, tomatoes, bell pepper, and basil leaves. (Alternately, place each ingredient on a separate skewer.) Place a slice of lemon at the end of each skewer to hold the seafood and vegetables in place and keep them from falling off the skewer. Place the finished skewers in a shallow broiler pan and pour the wine, oil, chopped basil, and salt and pepper to taste on top. Let marinate for at least 1 hour and up to 3 hours, covered and refrigerated.

3. Preheat the grill for high direct heat, 400 to 450 degrees F. Place a clean grill rack on the grill and let it get hot for about 3 minutes.

4. Remove the kebobs from the marinade, discarding the liquid. Cook the kebobs for about 5 minutes, gently flip them over, and cook for another 5 minutes on the other side. The scallops, shrimp, and swordfish should be cooked through, the tomatoes should be soft, and the bell peppers should still have a slight crunch. Serve hot.

GRILLED SALMON WITH PISTACHIO-LIME BUTTER

SERVES 2 TO 4

We love the way the lively flavors of this simple compound butter (fresh lime and crunchy pistachios) wake up the flavor of grilled salmon. Make the butter ahead of time (it can be covered and refrigerated for a full day) and you can have dinner on the table in well under an hour. Serve with basmati rice and a salad made from chopped summer vegetables.

If you want added flavor, you can cook the fish on a cedar (wood) plank instead of a fish rack.

INGREDIENTS

1½ pounds salmon fillet

1 tablespoon olive oil

1 teaspoon lime zest

Sea salt

Freshly ground black pepper

Pistachio-Lime Butter (page 43)

1 lime, cut into slices

1. Place the salmon in a nonreactive pan and coat with the oil, lime zest, and salt and pepper to taste. Let sit for 15 minutes.

2. Preheat the grill for medium-high direct heat, 325 to 375 degrees F. Place a clean grill rack on the grill and let it heat up for about 3 minutes.

3. Place the salmon on the grill rack, skin-side down, and cover. Cook for 10 minutes. Check the fish and, when you press down on the flesh with your finger and it doesn't feel raw, spoon the pistachio butter on top; cover the grill and cook for another 5 minutes. The salmon is done when it flakes easily and is opaque and hot, about 15 minutes total. Serve with the lime slices.

VARIATION

Use bluefish, haddock, cod, snapper, or any other firm-fleshed fish instead.

SWORDFISH TACOS WITH GREEN GUACAMOLE

SERVES 8

We weren't sure if swordfish—a firm, meaty fish—would work in a taco, but once we tried it, we were hooked! The fish is marinated briefly in lime juice, cilantro, olive oil, and coarse pepper and grilled until tender and juicy. Then we pile thin slices of the swordfish into warm tortillas (use the hot grill to heat them up) with salsa and guacamole. We also love making these tacos with fresh tuna steaks or any other firm fish.

INGREDIENTS

Two 1-pound swordfish steaks

¼ cup freshly squeezed lime juice

3 tablespoons finely chopped fresh cilantro

2 tablespoons olive oil

Coarsely ground black pepper

16 six-inch flour or corn tortillas

Green Guacamole (page 44) or your favorite guacamole

Mango Salsa (page 49) or homemade or store-bought salsa

8 leaves romaine or crunchy lettuce, coarsely chopped

1 lime, cut into wedges

Hot pepper sauce (optional)

1. Preheat the grill for high direct heat, 400 to 450 degrees F. Place a clean grill rack on the grill and let it get hot for about 3 minutes.

2. Put the fish in a nonreactive pan or bowl and coat it on both sides with the lime juice, cilantro, oil, and pepper to taste. Let it sit for 15 to 30 minutes. You don't want to marinate the fish much longer or the lime juice will start to "cook" the fish.

3. Remove the swordfish from the marinade. Grill the fish, covered, for 5 minutes on each side, or until tender when tested with a fork. Remove the fish from the grill and let sit for 1 minute. Heat the tortillas on the hot grill for about 1 minute per side.

4. Thinly slice the fish and serve with the warm tortillas, guacamole, salsa, lettuce, lime wedges, and hot pepper sauce, if desired. Let everyone put together their own tacos.

GRILLED SWORDFISH WITH OLIVE-SCALLION SALAD

SERVES 4

Here, we marinate swordfish steaks with herbs, olive oil, garlic, and coarse pepper and then grill them until tender. An olive salad, made with scallions and olive oil, is spooned on top for a delicious Mediterranean-style seafood dish.

INGREDIENTS

1½ pounds swordfish, tuna steak, or any firm seafood steak

2 tablespoons finely chopped fresh basil, rosemary, or thyme

1 tablespoon olive oil

1 clove garlic, minced

Coarsely ground black pepper

: : : : :

THE OLIVE-SCALLION SALAD

1 cup pitted black and green olives, coarsely chopped

¼ cup olive oil

2 scallions, finely chopped (white and green parts)

Coarsely ground black pepper

: : : : :

3 tablespoons freshly squeezed lemon juice

1 lemon, cut into wedges

1. Place the fish in a non-reactive pan or bowl and top with the herbs, oil, garlic, and pepper to taste. Marinate for at least 1 hour and up to 8 hours, covered and refrigerated.

2. *Make the olive-scallion salad:* In a small bowl, mix together the olives, oil, scallions, and pepper to taste and set aside. Cover and refrigerate if making ahead; *Continued...*

…continued

don't make more than 4 hours ahead of time.

3. Preheat the grill for high direct heat, 400 to 450 degrees F. Place a clean grill rack on the grill and let it get hot for about 3 minutes.

4. Remove the fish from the marinade, reserving the liquid. Place the swordfish on the grill, pour half of the lemon juice on top, cover, and cook for 4 minutes. Gently flip the fish over, baste with any extra marinade from the bowl and the remaining lemon juice, cover, and cook for another 4 to 5 minutes, depending on the thickness of the fish, or until just tender when lightly tested with a fork. Remove from the grill and place on a serving plate or platter. Spoon half of the olive salad on top and serve the remaining olive salad on the side with the lemon wedges.

GRILLED TUNA WITH GINGER-WASABI BUTTER

SERVES 4 TO 6

We like our tuna grilled hot on the outside and almost rare on the inside. Fresh tuna is seasoned with soy sauce, fresh ginger, sesame oil, and lemon juice; grilled; and then topped with a very simple ginger-and-wasabi-flavored butter sauce. Serve with a cold noodle salad and the Grilled Vegetable Platter (page 123).

INGREDIENTS

Two 1-pound tuna steaks

2 teaspoons sesame oil

1½ tablespoons soy sauce

1 tablespoon freshly squeezed lemon juice

1 teaspoon minced peeled fresh ginger

THE GINGER-WASABI BUTTER

4 tablespoons unsalted butter

3 tablespoons minced peeled fresh ginger

2 tablespoons prepared wasabi (see Note)

1½ tablespoons freshly squeezed lemon juice

1 tablespoon finely minced fresh chives

Freshly ground black pepper

1. Put the tuna in a non-reactive bowl or pan and cover with the oil, soy sauce, lemon juice, and ginger and marinate for at least 15 minutes and up to 30 minutes. You don't want the fish to sit longer or the lemon juice will start to "cook" the fish.

2. Preheat the grill for high direct heat, 400 to 450 degrees F. Place a clean grill rack on the grill and let it get hot for about 3 minutes.

Continued…

...continued

3. *Prepare the butter:*
Melt the butter in a small saucepan over low heat. Add the ginger and cook for 2 minutes. Mix in the wasabi and lemon juice and stir until smooth; cook for another 2 minutes. Stir in the chives and pepper to taste and set aside.

4. Remove the tuna from the marinade. Grill the tuna steaks, covered, for 3 minutes. Gently flip the tuna over and cook for another 2 to 5 minutes; 2 minutes will give you a rare center and 5 minutes will give you fish cooked to medium. Warm the butter on the grill or on the stove and spoon over the tuna. Serve hot.

NOTE
Wasabi powder can be found in Asian markets or in the specialty food aisles of most grocery stores. You simply mix 1 tablespoon of the powder with a touch of water to make a thick paste.

GRILLED VEGETABLE PLATTER

SERVES 6 TO 8

This recipe is surprisingly easy when you consider what an elegant, show-off kind of presentation it makes. We grill asparagus, bell peppers, onions, fennel, zucchini, leeks, and scallions and serve them all in a deep bowl or, alternatively, on a huge white platter with chimichurri sauce on the side. The colors, textures, and flavors of the vegetables make a great combination. You can serve them as a side dish or a main course, accompanied by a big salad and crusty bread.

The grilling times are approximate because it depends on the size, the freshness, and the thickness of the vegetables. The end result should be vegetables that have beautiful grill marks and are cooked until soft but not limp. You'll need a grill basket or rack to keep the vegetables from spilling through the grill grates.

INGREDIENTS

1 red onion, peeled and quartered	1 yellow bell pepper, cut into 1½-inch wedges
1 yellow onion, peeled and quartered	1 green bell pepper, cut into 1½-inch wedges
1 fennel bulb, trimmed, cored, and cut into 6 wedges	2 leeks, cut lengthwise in half or quarters (if large)
2 medium zucchini, ends trimmed and quartered lengthwise	6 scallions, ends trimmed
	½ cup olive oil
1 pound asparagus, ends trimmed	Sea salt
1 red bell pepper, cut into 1½-inch wedges	Freshly ground black pepper
	Chimichurri Sauce (page 50)

1. Put all the vegetables onto a rimmed baking sheet and sprinkle evenly with the oil, and salt and pepper to taste.

2. Preheat the grill for high direct heat, 400 to 450 degrees F. Place two clean grilling baskets or grill racks on the grill and let them get hot for about 3 minutes.

Continued...

...*continued*

3. Grill the onions and fennel for 5 to 7 minutes per side. Grill the zucchini for 4 to 6 minutes per side. Grill the asparagus and bell peppers for 5 minutes per side. Grill the leeks for 3 to 4 minutes per side.

Grill the scallions for 2 to 2½ minutes per side. To test for doneness, the vegetables should be tender but not limp. Serve the vegetables warm or at room temperature with the Chimichurri Sauce; they will hold up for several hours after grilling.

VARIATION

Add fingerling potatoes and follow the directions on page 28.

GRILLED JAPANESE-STYLE EGGPLANT

SERVES 4 TO 6

What we love about these grilled eggplant wedges is the gorgeous, almost lacquered color they take on and their smoky, slightly spicy, salty flavor. Serve them with barbecued meats or on top of rice.

INGREDIENTS

2 medium or 4 small globe eggplants (about 1½ pounds), trimmed and cut into 8 long thin wedges each

¼ cup kosher salt

½ cup soy sauce

2 scallions, finely chopped (white and green parts)

3 tablespoons minced peeled fresh ginger

2 tablespoons sesame oil

1 tablespoon Chinese chile paste (see page 108)

2 cloves garlic, minced

¼ cup coarsely chopped fresh cilantro

1. Cut small "Xs" into the flesh of the eggplant wedges, about 1 inch apart. Place the eggplant, flesh-side up, in a colander and sprinkle with the salt. Let sit in a sink for 30 minutes. (This will help reduce the moisture in the eggplant and remove bitter juices.) Rinse the salt off under running cold water and dry thoroughly.

2. Meanwhile, preheat the grill for medium-high direct heat, 325 to 375 degrees F. Place a clean grill rack or basket on the grill and let it get hot for about 3 minutes.

3. In a medium bowl, mix together the soy sauce, half of the scallions, the ginger, oil, chile paste, and garlic.

4. Using a barbecue brush or a pastry brush, lightly brush the eggplant skin with some of the marinade. Place the eggplant on the grill, skin-side down, cover, and let it cook for 5 minutes. Brush the flesh with the marinade and gently flip the eggplant over. Cover and let it cook for 5 minutes more. The eggplant should be getting soft. Generously brush the eggplant with

Continued...

. . . *continued*

the marinade again, flip it over once more, and cook for another 1 to 5 minutes, or until the eggplant is soft throughout and *almost* collapsed. Remove it to a platter and scatter it with the cilantro and remaining scallions. Serve hot or at room temperature with the remaining marinade on the side.

VARIATIONS

Sprinkle the finished dish very lightly with red chile flakes for a slightly spicy flavor.

Sprinkle the finished dish with dried bonito flakes, which are available in Asian markets.

Sprinkle the finished dish with lightly toasted sesame seeds.

GRILLED PIZZA: THE BASIC, WITH VARIATIONS ON A THEME

EACH PIZZA SERVES 2 TO 4

Grilling pizza sounds like it might be complicated, but it's so simple you'll become hooked. If you buy premade pizza dough, you can put the pizza together in very little time, depending on your toppings. Here, we offer a basic, classic Margherita pizza (grilled dough, fresh mozzarella, summer tomato slices, olive oil, and fresh basil), with many ideas for various other toppings. We want you to start with something simple so you can get comfortable with the basic technique, and then start experimenting.

INGREDIENTS

1 pound pizza dough (see Note)

Flour for rolling out the dough

4 tablespoons olive oil

2 ripe summer tomatoes, thinly sliced

Sea salt

Freshly ground black pepper

8 ounces fresh mozzarella, thinly sliced

¼ cup very thinly sliced fresh basil

1. Preheat the grill for high indirect heat, 400 to 450 degrees F.

2. Cut the dough in half. Working on a lightly floured surface, roll out one piece of dough until it's about 11 inches long and 8 inches wide. Lightly oil a rimmed baking sheet with about 1 tablespoon of the oil and place the dough on the oiled sheet. Repeat with the remaining dough.

3. Put the tomatoes and 1 tablespoon oil in a bowl; season with salt and pepper.

Put all your other toppings (in this case, the cheese and basil) into small bowls or on plates and bring them out to the grill with your dough.

4. Working with one piece of dough at a time, carefully use a wide spatula or pizza paddle and lift the dough from the baking sheet. Slowly slide the dough onto the hottest part of the grill for 2 minutes. Using tongs or a wide spatula, gently move the dough to the unheated section of the grill for 1 minute. This will give the dough good grill marks

and a nicely charred surface without burning it. The bottom side of the dough should look lightly cooked.

5. Gently flip the dough over and place it over the hot part of the grill again. Quickly and gently arrange half the cheese on top of your dough. Arrange half of the tomato slices on top, drizzling ½ tablespoon of the oil over the pizza. Scatter half of the basil on top and cover the grill. Let it cook for 2 minutes. Carefully pull the pizza over to the unheated part of the grill, cover, and let it cook for 2 to 4 minutes more, or until the dough puffs up slightly, looks cooked, and the cheese and toppings are melted and hot. Remove the pizza to a cutting board or platter and repeat with the remaining dough and toppings. Cut the pizzas into slices and serve hot.

NOTE

Look for premade pizza dough in the refrigerated section of your supermarket or ask your local pizza parlor if you can buy dough from them. You can also use your favorite homemade pizza dough recipe.

VARIATIONS

Scatter the pizza, hot off the grill, with 1 cup arugula leaves. The heat will just wilt the greens.

Grill 2 sweet or hot sausages for 5 to 8 minutes, depending on the thickness. Cut into thin slices and use as a topping.

Stir 2 large onions, very thinly sliced, in 2 tablespoons olive oil over very low heat for about 15 minutes, or until caramelized. Use as a topping.

Quarter fresh figs and thinly slice prosciutto and add instead of, or in addition to, the tomatoes and basil on the pizza.

Experiment with various cheeses: Use feta, Cheddar, goat, Parmesan, Gruyère, or others instead of, or in addition to, the mozzarella.

Add 1 cup pitted black or green olives.

Spread the crust of the pizza with 1 to 2 tablespoons tapenade and then place other fillings on top.

Scatter very thinly sliced or lightly sautéed garlic on the pizza.

Sprinkle with chile flakes for a slightly spicy flavor.

Sauté 1 pound baby spinach until just wilted. Place the spinach on the pizza over crumbled feta cheese and add pitted black olives.

Use sun-dried tomatoes instead of fresh when tomatoes are out of season.

3

CHAPTER

DESSERTS

BROWN SUGAR–CARAMELIZED PINEAPPLE WITH ICE CREAM

SERVES 4 TO 6

Pineapple has so much natural sugar that when you sprinkle it lightly with light brown sugar and grill it, an instant caramelization process occurs. The pineapple turns golden brown and incredibly sweet. We like to chop it into chunks and put it over vanilla or ginger ice cream. A sweet dessert in less than ten minutes!

INGREDIENTS

1 ripe pineapple, peeled, cored, and cut into ½-inch slices

About 1 cup packed light brown sugar

1 pint vanilla or your favorite ice cream

1. Preheat the grill for high direct heat, 400 to 450 degrees F.

2. Put the pineapple slices on a large plate or platter and press about 1 tablespoon of the sugar on top of each slice. Place the pineapple directly on the hot grill, sugar-side up, cover, and cook for 3 minutes. Gently flip the pineapple over and sprinkle another tablespoon of sugar on top of each slice. Cover and let cook for 3 minutes more. Gently flip the pineapple and cook for another minute; the pineapple should have nice grill marks and be a pale golden brown, and the sugar should have melted and caramelized on both sides. Remove from the heat. Cut into small chunks and serve on top of ice cream.

NOTE
Be careful the sugar doesn't drip and catch fire. Have a spray bottle of water to tame the flames if needed.

VARIATIONS
Add a pinch of ground ginger or cardamom to the brown sugar.

Brush on maple syrup or honey instead of the brown sugar.

GRILLED LIME AND MAPLE BANANAS

SERVES 2 TO 4

Is it a dessert or a side dish? You decide. We cut bananas in half lengthwise, grill them with fresh lime juice, and baste them with maple syrup and light brown sugar. The sugars caramelize and add a sweet flavor to the fresh citrus and banana. We love serving these hot bananas with scoops of vanilla or maple ice cream or as a side dish to barbecued pork, ribs, or seafood.

INGREDIENTS

2 large bananas

2½ tablespoons freshly squeezed lime juice

⅓ cup maple syrup

¼ cup packed light brown sugar

1. Peel the bananas and cut them in half lengthwise.

2. Preheat the grill for medium-high direct heat, 325 to 375 degrees F. Place a clean grill rack on the grill and let it get hot for about 3 minutes.

3. Drizzle the lime juice on the bananas. Grill the bananas, flat-side down, for 1 minute. Gently flip them over so the curved parts of the bananas are down. Baste the bananas with the maple syrup and sprinkle on the sugar. Cover and cook for 2 minutes. Baste with any remaining syrup and cook for 1 minute more, or until the sugars are caramelized. Serve hot.

GRILLED HONEY PEACHES

SERVES 4

This entire recipe takes ten minutes, making it an ideal dessert for summertime and grilling season. Cut a peach in half, brush it with good honey, and grill for five minutes. Serve with a dollop of crème fraîche or Greek yogurt and you've got a simple summer treat.

INGREDIENTS

4 ripe (but not too ripe) summer peaches, halved and pitted

About ⅓ cup good floral honey

1 cup crème fraîche, Greek-style yogurt, or sour cream

1. Preheat the grill for medium-high direct heat, about 325 to 372 degrees F. Place a clean grill rack or basket on the grill and let it get hot for about 3 minutes.

2. Bring a small pot of water to a simmer over high heat. Place the open jar of honey in the hot water and warm it until the honey becomes thin and pourable. Using a pastry brush or a grill brush, brush the skin side of the peaches with some of the honey. Place them on the hot grill, flesh-side down, cover, and cook for 2 minutes. Gently flip the peaches over so the skin side is down, and spoon a generous amount of honey into the peach cavities. Cover the grill and cook for another

3 minutes. The honey should caramelize on the peaches and the peach flesh should begin to turn a golden brown. The peaches should be slightly soft but not "cooked."

3. Place the peaches on a platter. Spoon a generous dollop of the crème fraîche alongside or into the cavity of each peach and drizzle the remaining honey on top.

VARIATIONS

Sprinkle with chopped toasted pistachios, pine nuts, or your favorite nut.

Decorate the plate with edible flower blossoms.

Substitute ripe summer nectarines, apricots, or plums for the peaches.

GREEK YOGURT PANNA COTTA WITH LEMON AND BLUEBERRIES

SERVES 6

Panna cotta (literally meaning "cooked cream") is traditionally made with cream, but we decided to lighten things up and substitute Greek-style yogurt and buttermilk. The result: panna cotta with the same fabulous silky texture, but way less fat. A subtle hint of lemon zest adds a wonderful summery flavor. Plan on letting the panna cotta sit in the refrigerator for at least four hours to firm up. Serve in the ramekins or unmold the panna cotta and surround it with blueberries or an assortment of summer berries.

INGREDIENTS

Butter for greasing ramekins

One 0.3-ounce packet unflavored gelatin

3 cups whole-fat plain Greek yogurt

1 teaspoon vanilla extract

1 cup buttermilk

½ cup sugar

1½ teaspoons lemon zest

About 2 cups blueberries, or any assortment of summer berries

1. Lightly grease six 8-ounce ramekins with butter and set aside.

2. Mix the gelatin and 3 tablespoons of cold water in a small heatproof bowl until the mixture has the consistency of applesauce, and set aside. Stir the yogurt and vanilla together in a large bowl, and set aside. Heat the buttermilk to a bare simmer in a small saucepan. (It may separate a little; that's okay.) Add the sugar and stir until dissolved. Remove the pan from the heat and set it aside.

3. Place the bowl with the gelatin mixture in a small skillet filled with about ½ inch of water. Set the skillet over low heat and stir the gelatin until it is warm, soft, and completely clear. Remove it from the heat and stir the gelatin into the pan with the buttermilk, then stir that mixture into the bowl with the yogurt mixture until completely smooth. Add the lemon zest and gently stir to make sure it's completely incorporated.

4. Divide the yogurt mixture among the ramekins, cover with plastic, and refrigerate until firm for at least 4 hours and up to 3 days. Serve in the ramekins or, using a warm kitchen knife, unmold the panna cottas from the ramekins onto small serving plates and surround them with the berries.

VARIATIONS

Drizzle Greek honey over the panna cotta.

Garnish the tops of the panna cottas with candied lemon peel or lemon zest.

Garnish the tops of the panna cottas with slivers of crystallized ginger.

INDEX

TABLE OF EQUIVALENTS

The exact equivalents in the following tables have been rounded for convenience.

LIQUID/DRY MEASUREMENTS	
U.S.	METRIC
¼ teaspoon	1.25 milliliters
½ teaspoon	2.5 milliliters
1 teaspoon	5 milliliters
1 tablespoon (3 teaspoons)	15 milliliters
1 fluid ounce (2 tablespoons)	30 milliliters
¼ cup	60 milliliters
⅓ cup	80 milliliters
½ cup	120 milliliters
1 cup	240 milliliters
1 pint (2 cups)	480 milliliters
1 quart (4 cups, 32 ounces)	960 milliliters
1 gallon (4 quarts)	3.84 liters
1 ounce (by weight)	28 grams
1 pound	448 grams
2.2 pounds	1 kilogram

LENGTHS	
U.S.	METRIC
⅛ inch	3 millimeters
¼ inch	6 millimeters
½ inch	12 millimeters
1 inch	2.5 centimeters

OVEN TEMPERATURES		
FAHRENHEIT	CELSIUS	GAS
250	120	½
275	140	1
300	150	2
325	160	3
350	180	4
375	190	5
400	200	6
425	220	7
450	230	8
475	240	9
500	260	10